Sermons for a Modern World

Sermons that Matter

Emily Hotho

Parson's Porch Books
www.parsonsporchbooks.com

Sermons for a Modern World
ISBN: Softcover 978-1-949888-76-8
Copyright © 2019 by Emily Hotho

All rights reserved. No part of this book may be reproduced or transmitted in any form or by any means, electronic or mechanical, including photocopying, recording, or by any information storage and retrieval system, without permission in writing from the publisher.

Sermons for a Modern World

Contents

Introduction 7

Part 1: Creative Series

How to Help: God Cares for Caregivers 11
    Psalm 63:1, Psalm 23:1-6, Colossians 3:23-24

When Christians Disagree: War and Peace 16
    Matthew 5:39-44

The Carols of Christmas: "O Little Town of Bethlehem" 21
    Micah 5:1-5, Matthew 2:1-8

Trending Topics: Adult Coloring Books 26
    Psalm 92:12-15

The Gospel on Broadway: Dear Evan Hansen 31
    Deuteronomy 31:1-6, Hebrews 13:1-5

Christianity &... Spiritual but not Religious 35
    Leviticus 26:12, Psalm 96:11-12
    1 Corinthians 12:7-12, 27

Christianity &... Scientology 41
    Romans 5:1-8

Part 2: Biblical Exegesis Sermons

Hang in There 49
    Revelation 1:1-11

Sing in the Storm 54
    Revelation 5:1-10

The Cursing Psalms 60
    Psalm 109

Peter: The Sequel (Acts 4)
    Acts 4:1-20 65

Send Me 70
    Isaiah 6:1-13

Jesus' Healing Ministry 75
    Mark 2:1-12

Part 3: Sermons Connecting with Children, Youth, and Young Adults

Young Adults: Do You Need Church? 83
   Ephesians 4:1-13

Faith Like a Child 89
   Luke 18:15-17

Part 4: Preaching Theological Topics

Why Did Jesus Have to Die? 97
   Romans 5:6-11

Zoom: Denomination (LGBTQIA+ Inclusion in The United Methodist Church) 103
   1 Corinthians 13:12-13

Part 5: Sermons for Holidays and Liturgical Seasons

Christmas Eve: Let Every Heart Prepare Him Room 113
   Revelation 3:20

Ash Wednesday: What God Can Do With Dust 116
   Isaiah 58:1-9

Easter Sunday: Believing the Resurrection 119
   Matthew 28:1-10

Part 6: Preaching Personally

Service of Death and Resurrection: Glenn Savage 127
   Isaiah 40:28-31

Your Move: Lead 130
   1 Corinthians 12:1-30

Service of Death and Resurrection: Art Brundage 136
   Psalm 84

Introduction

I have been a United Methodist pastor for 13 years. But only for the past six years have I been in a position that requires me to preach almost every single Sunday. My first appointment out of seminary was as an associate pastor of a large congregation with five clergy; I preached monthly if I was lucky. My next position was an administrative role on our Conference staff. And for the last six years, I have served as the pastor of Skycrest United Methodist Church, a vibrant mid-sized church in beautiful Clearwater, Florida.

It is both easier and harder to preach week in and week out. It is easier, in that you don't feel the need to say *everything*; you know you'll get another opportunity next week. It is harder, in that it feels like every time you turn around, another Sunday is coming, and quickly!

It is also deeply meaningful to preach each week to a congregation whom you love. Have you ever heard a congregant say, "Pastor, I felt like you were preaching directly to me today?" Well, sometimes we actually are. I don't know everything about my congregation, but I know a lot about their joys, struggles, temptations, and doubts. I do my best each week to listen to God on their behalf and preach accordingly.

The sermons in this book were preached to a particular congregation at a particular time. Much like reading the Pauline letters in Scripture is like reading someone else's mail, reading sermons is a bit like listening in to a particular conversation between a church and its pastor. But these sermons are also, hopefully, the gospel, good news for the world. And so I hope they will be meaningful for those beyond my church family as well as those within it.

This book is organized into six sections. In my particular tradition, you'll find pastors who preach the lectionary, and those who preach topical sermon series. I tend to do both; preaching more traditionally during Lent and Advent; and preaching more creatively during other times of the year. Parts 1 and 2 give a few examples of each.

As someone who began pastoral ministry at age 25, and now as a mom of three kids, I am passionate about young adults, youth, and children in the church. You'll see some of that reflected in the sermons in Part 3.

My favorite sermons to preach are funeral sermons, several of which you'll find in Part 6. I love getting to peek into someone's life, whether through knowing them personally or through the memories of their loved ones and find a common thread that leads to the gospel. More new members have come to Skycrest after attending one of our funerals than almost any other outreach or advertising that we do!

Whether you're a preacher, a church member, or just someone curious about the Christian faith, I hope you enjoy reading these sermons.

Part 1:
Creative Series

How to Help: God Cares for Caregivers
Psalm 63:1, Psalm 23:1-6, Colossians 3:23-24

For this sermon, I had three pitchers on stage. One full, one half-full, and one empty with a hole in it.

Imagine you're getting ready to board a flight. You get on, find your seat, turn your cell phone off, and buckle up. The flight attendants begin their pre-flight instructions, and if you are like me and most fliers, you tune them out. You have heard it all before; those instructions you almost certainly will never need to remember: "In the event you need oxygen during the flight, oxygen masks will descend from the overhead compartments. Put on your mask first before attempting to assist another person."

These instructions are not meant to be unkind. They are not self-centered. They are simply necessary to make sure you have oxygen before trying to assist someone else; otherwise it puts you both in danger.

This same principle holds true in life. We have to take care of ourselves if we are going to be able to help, care for, and serve the people around us. But that can be easier said than done.

I know many of you have taken care of an aging parent, a spouse struggling with an illness, a grandchild, or a loved one with special needs. If you never have, pay extra attention; it is very possible that someday you will be called on to care for someone who is unable to care for themselves.

There are at least 44 million adults providing care for an older or chronically ill family member, and even more people providing other types of care. Half of all caregivers only have to devote eight hours per week, but 20% of caregivers spend more than 40 hours a week giving care. Such care giving, on average, will last 4.3 years.[1]

---

[1] https://www.caregiver.org/caregiver-statistics-demographics

Care-givers are more likely than the general population to get infectious diseases. They are more susceptible to heart disease, arthritis, diabetes and cancer. And those tendencies hang around for years after a stint of care giving ends. Caregivers have a greatly increased risk for anxiety and depression. Sometimes they feel guilty for not being with some members of their families while they care for another. Other times they doubt or second-guess whether they're making the right decisions and doing all they can for the person in their care. That's a lot to deal with!

Surely God has something to say to these millions and millions of people who provide care to their loved ones in need. Surely God sees what many of you are doing and wants to encourage you and strengthen you and let you know you are not alone in this. Surely the Bible has some wisdom for this phase of life that so many of us are bound to find ourselves in today or someday.

I think what God has to say is, essentially, those pre-flight instructions. Put on your own mask before attempting to assist other people. We'll take a look at a couple of Psalms today that I think illustrate that perfectly.

The reason you need to put on your own mask first in a caregiving relationship is that it is not a reciprocal relationship. The other person isn't in a position to be able to help you with your mask. They are not equally able to reciprocate when care is needed in your life. They might be the most wonderful, incredible, loving person in the world, you might love them more than anything.... but in that situation, for that time, they are not able to give back to you in all the ways you need. It's not reciprocal. They are also not always necessarily able to thank you for your service in the way you deserve to be thanked. They are not necessarily able to show gratitude for all that you do. They are not always even able to be all that nice, cooperative, or pleasant while receiving your care.

When I was in fourth grade, I broke my leg and the bone had to be re-set in traction, so for a couple of weeks I was in the hospital while my leg hung there suspended by a metal pin through my knee. Sometimes at night my muscles would spasm, and my broken leg with a metal rod through it would shake uncontrollably, which was excruciatingly painful. My whole family remembers one night when that was happening, and the doctor came in to try and calm me down. He called me sweetheart and tried to pat me on the head. I screamed such awful things at him that he ended up just leaving the room! I was a small very shy 9-year-old girl. But in that moment, I was not able to be appropriately thankful, polite, or even nice to the doctor who was working so hard to provide me with care.

As care-givers, you simply cannot get your value or worth from the person you are caring for. It is—at least for the time that you are their caregiver—not a reciprocal relationship. They are not going to be reliably able to give back to you in terms of appreciation or help or sometimes even basic kindness, because of what they are going through.

As care-givers, you also cannot expect to get your value or worth from the outside world seeing all that you are doing. The reality is, much of what you do will go unseen and unnoticed by everyone. Except God.

There are plenty of times in my job when I go and visit and pray for people who may not be able to remember that I have visited them or prayed for them. I truly believe, theologically speaking, that it is important to go there on behalf of the church and pray and hold someone's hand, even if they don't know that I'm there. Even if they can't remember it and no one else sees it. But I will also tell you that there are times when I am frustrated that they can't remember it and no one else sees it.

One time I was planning a funeral with some family members and the spouse of the deceased had dementia. She kept asking for all the former pastors not only of our church, but of every Methodist church in Clearwater. As much as I knew and understood that she simply could not remember, a little part of me wanted to ask her, "What am I, chopped liver? I've visited you and your husband dozens of times, I've been your pastor for years, and now you want Michael or Joe or Chuck or whoever? That's not fair!"

Even the holiest among us would like to be noticed and appreciated. But as care-givers, the relationship is not reciprocal. It's not fair to expect to get our self-worth from the person we're serving, or the outside world, seeing us and thanking us.

It's like these pitchers of water. This one (half-full) is you. This one (empty) is the person you are caring for. You pour into them. But it's as if their pitcher has a hole in it (which is the illness, the struggle, whatever issue they're facing) and so they can't pour back into you right now. So now you're empty. And if you're relying on them to pour back into you with their thanks and kindness, even if you wouldn't say that out loud, if that expectation is somewhere deep in your soul…. you may be disappointed because there's a hole in their pitcher right now. They can't pour back.

But there's Someone who can.

READ PSALM 63:1

This Psalm is traditionally attributed to David while he was fleeing for his life due to a rebellion in Jerusalem; his trek led him to the desert where it is said that he wrote this prayer to God. Like most of the Psalms, we can't be certain of the origin, but we can tell that the person who wrote this prayer was all alone and didn't have anyone to pour into him, to fill his cup.

But then there's this other Psalm that shows us a different image.

READ PSALM 23:1-6

At the point in which this Psalm was written, the Psalmist had found a way to allow God to pour into his life, so that he was not empty, but overflowing.

How? How can God fill your cup? Well, that's kind of up to you to find out. It probably has some overlap with things you like or find relaxing. But it is not the same as just *anything* you like or find relaxing. It is things that connect you with God. Things that let you know that you are loved and valued by God. Things that God can use to give you rest and strength and joy to keep on caring for the person you've been given to care for. It might be coming to church or to a small group. It might be making time to talk with a friend or investing in getting a good counselor. It might be a hobby or something that's good for your health. It might be prayer or silence.

Your worth, security, and value must come from somewhere. The person you're caring for cannot bear that entire responsibility. Even your friends and family and community can't do it; they will fail you if you are relying on them alone to fill your cup. But God can.

And once God does, you will have more to give!

READ COLOSSIANS 3:23-24

God has poured into you, and now you go back and serve not only your loved one, but also God, with your caregiving. Martin Luther King Jr. said to a group of high school students:

If it falls your lot to be a street sweeper, sweep streets like Michelangelo painted pictures, sweep streets like Beethoven composed music, sweep streets like Shakespeare wrote poetry. Sweep streets so well that all the hosts of heaven and earth will have to pause and say: Here lived a great street sweeper who swept his job well.[2]

Or, here lives a great caregiver who cared for a person well.

When you serve not just the person but God, you're not ridden with guilt or bitterness. It is a joy to serve God, who has poured so much into you. It is a joy to serve God whose image is in this person you're caring for. And then you take time away for God to pour back into you, and then you serve again, not just the person, but God in the person. Until all the cups are running over.

---

[2] Martin Luther King Jr., "What Is Your Life's Blueprint," speech given to Barrett Junior High School, 1967. https://projects.seattletimes.com/mlk/words-blueprint.html

When Christians Disagree: War and Peace
Matthew 5:39-44

College football has wrapped up. The Super Bowl is coming. March Madness is right around the corner. I like sports okay; I don't mind watching them. I'm not really passionate about any of them, but I don't mind watching a little bit of any sport. But here's my big problem when I watch. There's really no team or player that I like any more than any other. I just cannot make myself care who wins! Even teams of cities I've lived in, schools I went to, I just honestly do not care if they win the game or not. So, here's what happens I always cheer for the team who's hitting. Or shooting. Or on offense. Whatever the sport may be, I cheer for whoever's trying to score. And then when they switch sides, because I don't actually care or have any loyalties, I have a hard time cheering against the other team ("stop them," "don't let them score," "don't make it"—that's hard to do if you don't really care) so I end up switching and cheering for the team who is now on offense. It annoys the people that I'm watching with; they don't have such an easy time switching perspectives, because they have deep-seated loyalties and passions about their teams. Because of how much they care, they can't just easily switch and see things from the other side. If you're a sports fan, maybe you can relate.

The same thing is true, too, of much bigger issues than sports. Political issues, ethical issues, faith issues. The more you care, the bigger the issue, the harder it is to see something from the other team's side.

And that can lead to conflicts. In our families, friendships, and workplaces. On social media. Maybe around the table at Christmas dinner. Conflict in itself isn't necessarily bad, but it can lead to things that are bad, like unkindness and broken relationships if we don't handle it well.

Sometimes we see an issue differently than someone, even if that someone is within our own family of faith, a brother or sister in Christ, who also believes they've arrived at their viewpoint biblically. You not only think you're right; you think you're on God's side of the issue. You not only support your team; you think you're on God's team. And so does the other person.

That's what we're going to be talking about in this sermon series, "When Christians Disagree." Each week I'll take one issue and spend about half the sermon talking about one side, the biblical basis behind it, why people think Christian faith supports that view. And then we'll spend the other half of the sermon on the other side of the issue, the biblical basis behind it and why people think Christian faith supports their view. You'll hear one issue from two biblical perspectives.

The idea here is that taking a look at both sides of an issue can help us grow in faith. Sometimes it can strengthen our own viewpoint, other times it can open our eyes to change. Most importantly, it can help us to learn more about the Bible and how we apply it, which is vitally important. And it can show us how to disagree while still loving one another.

Our issue for today is war and peace. Jesus said in his Sermon on the Mount:

READ MATTHEW 5:39-44

From the very beginning, probably from the very day that Jesus first said this, people have disagreed over what he meant.

Some interpret this Scripture to mean that Jesus-followers cannot support or be a part of war or violence in any way. Do not resist. Turn the other cheek. Love and pray for enemies but nothing else.

Christian pacifists look elsewhere in Scripture, too. Isaiah 2:4 reads "They shall beat their swords into plowshares and their spears into pruning hooks, nation shall not lift up sword against nation, neither shall they study war anymore." That's considered to be the ideal of God's kingdom, pacifists say, so why not try to live that way now. Or how about the commandment, "Thou shalt not kill" (Exodus 20:13). They also look to the New Testament: in Matthew 26:52, when Peter had cut off the ear of one of the servants who was arresting Jesus, Jesus said, "Put your sword back in its place; those who live by the sword die by the sword." Then there's the entire example of Jesus himself; he didn't resist arrest or fight back against those who were crucifying him, even though he could have. Instead he suffered willingly. He redeemed the violence done to him and turned it into good to reconcile us to God and each other. Then there's this whole idea in Scripture of the body of Christ, how faith makes us family in a way that is bigger than other things that might divide us like what country we are from. Pacifists would say love, self-sacrifice, laying down life, reconciliation, and peace seem to be prevailing values of Jesus and the Bible.

There are Christian pacifists who have held this view from the ancient church up through today: Tertullian, Hippolytus, Martin of Tours, who said, "I am a soldier of Christ, I cannot fight in the wars of man."[3] There are entire Christian denominations, like Quakers and Anabaptists, that hold non-violence as an essential value. Martin Luther King Jr. taught the power of non-violent resistance. "To our most bitter opponents we say: 'We shall match your capacity to inflict suffering by our capacity to endure suffering. We shall meet your physical force with soul force. Do to us what you will, and we shall continue to love you.'"[4]

That's Christian pacifism; that is one way to take the words of Jesus.

Other Christians look at those same words of Jesus about loving our neighbor, and they wonder what to do if one neighbor is mistreating another neighbor, or if a dictator is mistreating a whole country full of neighbors? What if some of my innocent neighbors are in danger at the hands of some dangerous person with a weapon, and we have the chance to do something about it? Some Christians would say there are times, when peaceful alternatives have failed, that war or violence is the best way we can love our neighbors who may be in danger.

Just like the pacifists, these folks, too, are getting their viewpoints from the Bible. They look at the Old Testament and notice how God sure did a lot of work through militaries and wars. Plus, there are positive war-like images in the Bible, even in the New Testament: "Put on the full armor of God" (Ephesians 6:11). Paul called Timothy a "good soldier of Jesus Christ" (2 Timothy 2:3). Those seem like odd metaphors to use in the Bible if violence is always a bad thing. Military

---

[3] https://sojo.net/articles/when-soldiers-become-saints
[4] https://kinginstitute.stanford.edu/king-papers/documents/loving-your-enemies-sermon-delivered-dexter-avenue-baptist-church

heroes like Gideon, Barak, Samson, and David are praised in the New Testament (Hebrews 11:32-24). Plus, there are instances in Scripture where Jesus, John the Baptist, Paul each interacted with soldiers and didn't tell them to leave their job. In Luke 7, Jesus healed the soldier's servant and when Jesus left the guy's house, Jesus didn't command the soldier to quit his job. He said, "I have not found such great faith in all of Israel" (Luke 7:9).

Saint Augustine, along with others, starting in the fourth century, helped to develop some ideas on what constitutes a "just" or righteous use of war or violence.
1. Must be waged by a proper authority
2. Only if peaceful attempts have all failed and war is a last resort
3. The cause and the motive must be just (protection of the innocent), not selfish
4. Must be a reasonable chance of success, not doing more damage than good
5. Civilians are not a reasonable target
6. Only use as much force as necessary to establish peace

Those who believe in this just war theory would say that if we can really use war, weapons, and violence in these ways, we will be fulfilling what Paul talked about in Romans 12:21: "Do not be overcome by evil but overcome evil with good." There are Christians from the ancient church until now who have believed that.

I think of all the people I know who have served in the military. Veterans, and even prisoners of war, from our own congregation; they have put their lives at risk because they truly believe they are helping to overcome evil with good. I think of those I know who have gotten the necessary training to carry a weapon and I sincerely trust that they have done so because they want to be in a position to save lives, protect the innocent, and overcome evil with good.

And I think of those whom I know who are pacifists, who truly believe that they can best live the words of Jesus by prioritizing peace over violence, at all times, even at risk to themselves and in that way overcome evil with good.

What can we take away from this today?

First, its hard applying the teachings of Jesus to everyday life. We've had these teachings of Jesus for two thousand years, and theologians still have differences in how we apply them to real life. I don't want to just flippantly assume that I should believe what my parents or a political party or a teacher told me to. I want to study, pray, struggle, hear from others and spend a lifetime figuring out what the teachings of Jesus mean for me.

Next, this goes so much deeper than how I vote, or what I say in a political discussion. Whatever ethic of peace and force I say I believe in, has an impact on my everyday life.

What help am I offering to those most likely to be affected by war or weapons: refugees, people in war-torn countries, and people in communities more likely to be affected by violence?

When do I lay down my will, and put peace and reconciliation first in my own life?

When do I stand up for an innocent victim and use whatever power God has given me to resist evil or help a neighbor?

What do I teach my kids about when to be peaceful and when to fight for what is right?

Are my words, my attitudes, and my life in keeping with my best understanding of what Jesus taught about peacefulness and the right use of force?

No matter which side I agree with, that's a lifetime's worth of work to do.

The Carols of Christmas: "O Little Town of Bethlehem"

Micah 5:1-5, Matthew 2:1-8

This sermon was preached on the fourth Sunday of Advent, on which we light the candle of Love.

In the late 1860's, the Reverend Phillips Brooks, one of the most dynamic and inspirational preachers in all of America, was burnt out. After the Civil War and then the assassination of President Lincoln, he had lost his fervor and couldn't recover.

So Rev. Brooks asked his church for a sabbatical and took a trip to the Holy Land. As part of that trip, he took a ride on horseback from Jerusalem to Bethlehem on the night of Christmas Eve. Brooks wrote about worship at that midnight service at the Church of the Nativity, built on top of the supposed actual site of Jesus birth: "I remember standing in the old church in Bethlehem, close to the spot where Jesus was born, when the whole church was ringing hour after hour with splendid hymns of praise to God, how again and again it seemed as if I could hear voices I knew well, telling each other of the Wonderful Night of the Savior's birth."[5]

When he returned, he wanted some way to express the presence of God he felt on that night, and so he wrote a poem:

O little town of Bethlehem
How still we see thee lie
Above thy deep and dreamless sleep
The silent stars go by
Yet in thy dark streets shineth
The everlasting light
The hopes and fears of all the years
Are met in thee tonight.

---

[5] https://www.umcdiscipleship.org/resources/history-of-hymns-o-little-town-of-bethlehem

Once he had completed the (then) five-verse poem, Rev. Brooks asked his organist, who was also his Sunday School leader, to compose a melody for his words. Lewis Redner, the organist, wracked his brain but kept coming up with nothing, until the Saturday night before the Sunday School children were supposed to learn the song. Late that night, he says it was like an angel awoke him, with the melody we know and love today as the tune to "O Little Town of Bethlehem", and he quickly filled in the harmony before heading to church that morning. He says, "neither Rev. Brooks or I thought the carol or the music to it would live beyond that Christmas, 1868."[6] But a nearby bookshop printed it on leaflets, and then another pastor included it in his Sunday School hymn-singing book and somehow it spread from there.

There was a fifth verse to the carol, which was eventually omitted, that seems directed to children, which makes sense knowing that the song was originally written for a Sunday School group.

Where children pure and happy
Pray to the blessed Child,
Where misery cries out to thee,
Son of the undefiled;
Where charity stands watching
And faith holds wide the door,
The dark night wakes, the glory breaks,
And Christmas comes once more.

If you have friends from England, they sing an entirely different tune to "O Little Town of Bethlehem."

(At this point in the sermon I sung a line of the carol to the alternate tune, Forest Green.)

I don't like it sang that way at all! Well turns out the Brits don't like it our way, either; British hymnologist Erik Routley has described the

---

[6] https://www.umcdiscipleship.org/resources/history-of-hymns-o-little-town-of-bethlehem

American melody to "O Little Town of Bethlehem" as "broken-backed and paralytic."

But I like our version of this song. Written for a bunch of children. Written the night before it was due. They didn't even think it would ever be sung by anyone outside their little church that year. Written by a man who was struggling to find his faith once again, who found it, in the little town of Bethlehem.

While most hymns and worship songs are addressed to God, or perhaps to the worshipers, "O Little Town of Bethlehem" is a song sung to a town! It was as if something about this little town helped the author to regain his faith, and maybe can help us, too.

The opening phrase of the hymn, "O Little Town of Bethlehem" is based on Scripture.

READ MATTHEW 2:1-8

This is a reference to Micah, a prophet from the Old Testament, who prophesied during a time when Israel and Judah were in a civil war, and then Israel was attacked by the Assyrians. Micah was writing to God's people in the southern kingdom of Judah, and he prophesied that somehow, someday, a leader would come from Bethlehem who would lead God's people into a time of security and peace.

READ MICAH 5:1-5a

When I was in seminary, I was assigned an internship to go and learn practical experience as a pastor. Duke University is a hub of education, medicine, and research, and the Raleigh-Durham area is known for business and technology. But most everything else surrounding it is rural, small-town, and southern. I was assigned as an intern to Bahama United Methodist Church, which I thought at first meant I was going to the Bahamas. But no, I was going to Bahama, an unincorporated area about 45 minutes north of Durham with a population of several hundred. There was one stop sign in the town. Not even a stop light, but a stop sign. And the men of the town would bring their folding chairs and their coffee and sit at the stop sign in the mornings, sharing the town gossip for the day. There were no stores, no restaurants, and no downtown. There was the church, the firehouse, the post office, and the stop sign.

Bethlehem was a similarly unimpressive place at the time when Jesus was born. It had a population of maybe 150. It was a quiet shepherding community. It was so small that it was left off of several lists of Judean cities found elsewhere in the Bible.

It did have some history, though. In Genesis 35, we read that Rachel died in Bethlehem. She died giving birth to Jacob's youngest son; she asked the midwife to name him Ben-Oni (son of my sorrows); but Jacob named him Benjamin (son of my right hand). Interestingly, Jesus would come to be known as both "a man of sorrows" and the son at the right hand of God. Bethlehem was where Ruth and Boaz (direct ancestors of Jesus) got together. And Bethlehem was where David, Israel's greatest king, was born and anointed.

And seven hundred years before Jesus was born, Micah prophesied that a ruler like David would come from the little town of Bethlehem once again.

God seems to love using the small, the insignificant, the lowly, to accomplish great things. Small things like the little town of Bethlehem. Small things like a poor carpenter and a young teenage mom. Small things like a baby born in a stable. Small things like that baby growing up and preaching a message of a different kind of kingdom.

Twenty-five years ago, it was a slow news day in Clayton, Delaware. A reporter noticed a small weed, actually a small sprout of a Douglas fir tree (probably an errant seed from a nearby Christmas tree farm) growing in a crack along the interstate.

The paper printed that photograph, along with the title "O Christmas Weed" and a sweet little fable about how all the little seed ever wanted to be was a Christmas tree. After this picture was in the paper the Department of Transportation demanded that the little seedling be removed immediately; it was a road hazard after all. But the people of Clayton rallied around their Christmas weed, bringing little decorations, tinsel and ornaments. The original Christmas weed has, of course, long since come and gone, some have died, some have been removed by the authorities, some have been stolen by thieves. But each year the people of Clayton put out a Christmas weed along the turnpike, decorate it, and station volunteers to watch over it and keep it safe for the Christmas season.[7]

Why do they care so much about a weed that grew in the crack along the side of the road? I think it reminds them that Christmas isn't about the 10-foot tree or the perfect décor or the best presents or parties or having the perfect family moments.

Christmas is about a God who used something small—a baby born in the little town of Bethlehem—to do something great—bring the whole world back to God.

---

[7] https://www.delawareonline.com/story/life/2018/12/18/readers-ask-us-run-christmas-weed-fable/2270672002/

Trending Topics:
Adult Coloring Books
Psalm 92:12-15

When we flew to Ohio last week to visit my family, I noticed something a little strange on the airplane. People were coloring. Not children, adults! There were numerous adults in the airport and on the plane, who pulled out a coloring book and a box of colored pencils or markers, and colored. Have you heard of this? Apparently the first adult coloring books were published in 2012, but the trend has absolutely taken over in the last year or so. Crayola just launched a set of markers, colored pencils, and adult coloring books in their line called Coloring Escapes last month. Researchers, art therapists, everyone from Johns Hopkins University to Yoga Magazine are touting adult coloring books as a great alternative to meditation with a lot of the same benefits. The act of coloring in these very intricate designs allows your brain to switch off from other thoughts and focus only on the moment. And being completely focused on the present moment is an antidote for the stress and anxiety of our fast-paced, multi-tasking world.

The fact that these coloring books are flying off the shelves tells us what we really already know. People are stressed out. Overwhelmed. Overworked. Too busy. Filled with anxiety, more than ever. Maybe you feel that way. I know I feel that way sometimes.

What's fascinating is that from the beginning of time, it seems, people have been getting stressed out, overwhelmed, overworked, busy, and anxious. What's even more fascinating is that God seemed to understand, from the very beginning of time, that we were going to get stressed out, overwhelmed, overworked, busy, and anxious. From the very beginning of time, God gave us a commandment, not a suggestion or a nice idea but an actual commandment, about how to pattern our time, by dividing it into work, and worship and rest.

It's called Sabbath. And before we jump right to applying this to our lives, we're going to take a look back at Scripture and tradition and learn a little more about it. So, the word Sabbath or Shabbat is the

Hebrew name for the seventh day of the week, which, in the Jewish calendar, is Saturday. From the very beginning of Scripture for both Jews and Christians, we get this idea of work and rest. It is found in the creation story itself, in which God created for six days and then rested on the seventh. If God is all-powerful, then did God need to rest? No! God wasn't tired. God doesn't get achy knees or a worn-out back. God worked and rested in order to show us the pattern of work and rest.

Just a little bit later in the Scripture, for both Jews and Christians, in the book of Exodus, Moses gets the Ten Commandments from God. The fourth one of those commandments is to honor the Sabbath and keep it holy. And then in Exodus 20:10, again, we are given the command "You shall not do any work on the Sabbath." Try to take your minds way back to ancient times. Ancient civilization didn't work Monday through Friday, 9:00 A.M. to 5:00 P.M. They didn't clock in to work; they worked to survive. There wasn't a weekend. To take one day in seven to rest from work was a huge act of trust in God. They were willingly working less, earning less, because they trusted God to take care of them. It illustrated that God loves us out of grace, not because of how much we produce or achieve. It demonstrated that it's not us who keep the world spinning, but God.

Jews, particularly the Orthodox branch, took very seriously figuring out exactly how to honor the Sabbath and keep it holy. They spelled out the rules in the *Talmud*, which is their secondary Scripture. You can't turn on a light-switch on the Sabbath. You cannot write or build or hunt or sew or drive or cook. You can't separate wheat from chaff; and therefore, by extension, you cannot pick bones out of fish: gefilte fish is their solution to that. All of that to say, Jewish people take it very seriously to completely pause from working and creating for a day, in order to remind themselves that God is God, and we're not.

We know from the New Testament that Jesus practiced Sabbath, though he was willing to break some of the specific rules in order to heal or help people in need. When the Pharisees scolded Jesus for doing this, he replied that "the Sabbath was made for man, not man for the Sabbath" (Mark 2:27). Still, Jesus regularly took time away to rest, to stop working, and refresh his spirit.

In the religion class I teach at the college, one of the questions on the final exam is to explain why Jews have their Sabbath on Saturdays, and Christians on Sundays. Saturdays were considered the seventh day of the week, so that's when Jews believe God commanded them to rest. But Jesus was raised from the dead on a Sunday, so Christians practice Sabbath (rest and worship) on Sundays. So, for Christians, Sabbath represents rest, and also worship, and also new life. That's the difference between Sabbath and time off, self-care, or "me time". The recipient of "me time" is me. The recipient of self-care is me. The recipient of Sabbath is both me and God.

If Sabbath is from God, practiced by Jesus, and good for us, why do we resist it? And I can tell you, at times, I resist, avoid, and miss out on Sabbath, just as much as you do.

Because the rest of the world does not Sabbath and we need to keep up; there are kids' sports, birthday parties, things to be done, work, all weekend long. We keep a family calendar at home and a couple weeks ago we took a look at May and it had all this white space on it. And as much as we vowed to try to keep it that way, May no longer looks like a lot of white space. One reason we don't do Sabbath is because the world doesn't do Sabbath and we feel like we need to keep up.

Another reason I struggle with Sabbath is because I, like many others, like the "easy rest" of television, social media, restaurants, or strolling the mall. It seems like work to pray, read the Bible, sit in silence, or spend quality time in relationships.

We struggle with Sabbath also because church can cause busyness, with obligations to attend numerous events, or serve in multiple ministries. It's hard to find that balance, because serving is important, too, and a lot of the opportunities to serve are on Sundays! So maybe it means that you help with Sunday School during one time slot, and you attend service during the other. Or maybe you love leading music, but occasionally you go to the other service where you can just sit quietly in the back and worship. Even I take Fridays off; and I don't work every single Sunday and sometimes I go to a Saturday night service where I am only worshiping and not working.

Those are a few reasons we struggle with Sabbath; maybe you've got your own. But if we keep going at the same pace without a habit of regular Sabbath, for weeks, months, or years, we will inevitably end up in trouble.

What does God call us *not* to do on the Sabbath? Work. Multi-task. Worry. Be distracted.

What does God call us *to* do on the Sabbath? Things that remind you that God is God, that the world can keep running without your anxious hovering over it. Worship. Prayer. Spiritual reading. Cultivating relationships.

Psalm 92 is a poem or song in the Bible. The book of Psalms contains 150 of these poetic writings that span a lot of years and a lot of topics. Psalm 92 is the only one with a sub-heading that says, "for the Sabbath." It's a song praising God. And this is how it ends.

READ PSALM 92: 12-15

I love that end part about the tree. Trees don't grow just anywhere. Or, they might for a little while, but not if they're going to survive into old age. They have to be planted by a source of water and nourishment. They have to be cultivated.

Every pastors' meeting I attended when I was first starting out would go something like this. They would be talking to us about Sabbath, caring for ourselves, being in a group where we were being helped, not just giving help. And they would say, look to your left, look to your right. By the time you will reach retirement, one in three of you won't be here. Some of you will commit some kind of moral failure. Some of you will lose your faith. Some of you will burn out and leave the church. Some of you will find anxiety or depression worsening. (Sabbath alone doesn't typically cure those very real illnesses, but burnout can certainly contribute to them.) Some of you will actually die an early death exacerbated by stress. They told us the one differentiating factor they had seen was not talent or skill. It was Sabbath.

Ten years into it I think of the group I was ordained with, and I've seen almost all of these things happen. Moral failures, burnout, loss of faith. And this isn't just a thing for pastors; it is not about leaving ministry, it's about missing out on the good path God has for each of us because we would not obey God's command to honor one day in seven, to stop working so that God can work in us. Sabbath plants us by the waters that will keep us growing and refreshed and restored. Skipping Sabbath is like trying to grow a tree in a wasteland.

Would you think this week about what kind of Sabbath God is calling you to observe? Maybe you've got young kids and a leisurely morning at church followed by a Sunday nap and some spiritual reading is just not reality for you. Maybe you're very lonely and all of that open-ended resting time sounds anxiety-producing for you. Would you pray this week about how you could take one day in seven to stop working, worrying, multi-tasking, and being distracted, and take on something that reminds you that God is God, and God's got this world under control.

The Gospel on Broadway: Dear Evan Hansen
Deuteronomy 31:1-6, Hebrews 13:1-5

Broadway musicals are having a bit of a moment right now. Not just *Hamilton*, but also TV shows like *Glee* and movies like *La La Land*, live action musicals on television like last Easter's *Jesus Christ Superstar*, musicals like *Les Miserables* and *Into the Woods* as major big-screen releases. Musicals are everywhere lately.

These musicals are popular because the stories and songs resonate with people; you watch or listen to the soundtrack and you think, "I've felt that, I've experienced that."

We are doing something very special this month; we are partnering with *Not Your Normal Entertainment Company* to provide special music from four hit musicals. Then, in each sermon, we'll be exploring what in this musical people are connecting with, and what that tells us about the human experience that we can then connect to our faith as Christians.

Today, *Dear Evan Hansen*. This is a new musical that came out only a couple of years ago, won a bunch of Tony awards and made it into the Top 10 of the Billboard Music charts, something a cast recording of a musical almost never does.

The story begins on the first day of senior year of high school for two lonely teenage boys, Evan Hansen, who struggles with social anxiety, and Connor Murphy, a troubled loner bad-boy. They're not friends, neither one really has any friends, but they run into each other that day. Evan is in the computer lab printing out a letter he had to write to himself as an assignment from his therapist- "Dear Evan Hansen…" After an altercation, Connor ends up taking the letter. A few days later, Connor dies from suicide, and was found with the letter in his pocket, which everyone assumes was a suicide note addressed to Evan.

Connor's parents seem comforted to think that Connor had a close friend; so Evan goes along with it, creating a whole back-story of his friendship with Connor complete with post-dated emails to prove that the two were close. Evan grows closer with Connor's parents, even starts dating Connor's sister, and finds popularity and purpose at school as he takes the lead on "The Connor Project" in memory of his "friend." His whole life changes for the better because of this lie.

At the end of Act One, Evan gives this moving speech at a school assembly in memory of Connor:

(At this point in the sermon, a performer from the entertainment company we partnered with sang "You Will Be Found," from Dear Evan Hansen.)

Evan's speech goes viral on social media; he's gone from a nobody to an internet celebrity. And the audience goes into intermission thinking, wow, what a great message that you are not alone, but isn't this whole thing based on a lie? The "Dear Evan Hansen" note wasn't Connor's suicide note; they weren't even friends. Will everyone find out the truth? Do we want them to?

I won't spoil Act Two for you by telling you how it all plays out with Evan's big lie. What I'm interested in for today is the deeper truth in that song, in the story that this musical tells, and how it has struck a chord with so many people who are feeling alone.

In Genesis 2:18, when God was creating the earth, God says, "It is not good for man to be alone." That was as true when there was one person on this planet as it is when there are six billion. It is not good for man to be alone.

And yet many of us feel alone, perhaps more alone than ever. A newly-released public health survey shows that about half of Americans identify themselves as lonely, stating that they experience regular, ongoing loneliness and isolation. Young people are the age group with the highest rate of loneliness. The U.S. Surgeon General has chimed in on this loneliness epidemic, citing that it's as bad for your life span as smoking 15 cigarettes a day.[8] Great Britain just appointed a government official to deal with this crisis, a "minister of loneliness."[9]

Dear Evan Hansen has become so popular, not so much because of the songs or the acting or the set design, though they're all amazing. But because of the story. Because it tells people who feel lonely, "you are not alone," it tells people who feel lost, "you will be found."

There is another story that tells people that they are not alone. The Scriptures. This story says, "I will be with you always, even to the end of the age" (Matthew 28:20). It says, "Fear not, for I am with you, I have called you by name" (Isaiah 43:1). It says, "I no longer call you servants, but friends" (John 15:15). Pick a page and you'll see the message there: You are not alone. You will be found.

In Deuteronomy in the Old Testament, when God's people were almost done with their 40 years in the desert and they were about to cross over into the Promised Land, Moses knew that he would not be the one to lead them, Joshua would. Moses knew that Joshua would feel afraid and alone. He knew the people would feel afraid and alone. So he said this:

READ DEUTERONOMY 31:1-3, 6

You are not alone. You will be found. God will be with you.

One really interesting thing about the Bible is that the people writing the New Testament had the Old Testament as their Scripture, so they quote it quite a bit. They knew it really well, and their audiences that they were writing to also knew the Old Testament really well. So it is fascinating to see what they choose to quote from the Old Testament along with whatever point they're trying to make in the New Testament.

---

[8] https://www.washingtonpost.com/news/on-leadership/wp/2017/10/04/this-former-surgeon-general-says-theres-a-loneliness-epidemic-and-work-is-partly-to-blame/?utm_term=.b6753976ac6f
[9] https://www.nytimes.com/2018/01/17/world/europe/uk-britain-loneliness.html

The book of Hebrews is a New Testament letter written to Jewish converts to Christianity. The author wraps up his advice to them, quoting Deuteronomy 31.

READ HEBREWS 13:1-3, 5

So because God doesn't leave you or forsake you, don't leave or forsake one another. Because God is with you, be with each other. Love each other. Show hospitality to strangers. Remember those in prison as if you yourself were in prison, be with the suffering as if you yourself were suffering. Because God has not left you alone, do not leave one another alone. Because God has found you, find each other.

An elementary school student named Christian Rucks was told that his family would be moving to Germany for his dad's job. Christian was understandably nervous about being the new kid at a new school in a new country. But in researching schools with his mom online, he saw one school that had a "Buddy Bench," a designated place on the playground where a child could sit if they were feeling lonely, instead of slinking off alone, to be where another kid would see them and invite them to play. Christian's family didn't end up moving to Germany after all, and he brought the idea of the "Buddy Bench" to his principal in Roundtown, Pennsylvania, and from there the concept has spread to schools all around America.[10]

There is no "Buddy Bench" in life, though. Right? There's no clear place for people to show up and say, I'm lonely. I'm hurting. I'm lost. Someone notice me.

Unless maybe we are in such a place right now. Maybe the church is meant to be that kind of a place.

Because God has not left you alone, do not leave one another alone. What if church was like a buddy bench? What if church was like a beautiful musical that tells people that they aren't alone. Because God has found you, go find each other.

---

[10] https://www.yorkdispatch.com/story/news/2018/05/09/honored-central-student-creator-buddy-bench-shakes-presidents-hand/591401002/

Christianity &... Spiritual but not Religious
Leviticus 26:12, Psalm 96:11-12,
1 Corinthians 12:7-12, 27

When I get into a conversation with someone on an airplane, or at the gym, or at a coffee shop, eventually the question comes up, "What do you do?" Sometimes I try to avoid this question because it can get awkward, but, if they ask there's really no way around it, so I tell them, "I'm a pastor." After their initial surprise and a quick mental scan back through the last five minutes of conversation to make sure they didn't say any curse words, they then usually tell me about their own faith. Sometimes they tell me they are Baptist or Jewish or Presbyterian. But many times, I would say a large percentage of people I meet out in the community say, "Oh, I'm spiritual but not religious." They go on to explain that they believe in some sort of a God, that maybe they even believe in Jesus, but that they do not feel the need to go to church, read the Bible, or follow an organized pattern of prayer or spiritual disciplines. "I find God in watching a sunset at the beach," they say, "or in the eyes of my children or grandchildren." "I talk to God," they say, "I just don't have any need for organized religion."

Do you know someone like this? Spiritual but not religious? Or maybe *you* are spiritual but not religious, and someone convinced you to come today.

Up to one quarter of U.S. adults defined themselves in a recent study by Pew Research Forum as 'spiritual but not religious.'[11] Today we're going to take a closer look at what people mean when they say that. Why? Because, as Christians, anything that a fourth of our country is saying that they believe is worth understanding. We're going to do that today by looking at five characteristics of the spiritual but not religious and talk about each one.

---

[11] https://www.pewresearch.org/fact-tank/2017/09/06/more-americans-now-say-theyre-spiritual-but-not-religious/

First, people who call themselves spiritual but not religious mean that they connect with God privately rather than in corporate or public spaces. They say: "I don't need to go to church, I can talk to God anytime." Or "I connect with God best during my individual time of running, walking, or meditating; not at an organized activity like a church service."

The good? It is great to connect with God individually. Most Christians, myself included, could benefit from praying and worshiping more individually, instead of relying so heavily on one hour on Sundays.

The bad? God promises that we can experience God in a unique way in the church, in a worshiping community of people. If you say, "I don't need that" you're missing out.

Leviticus is arguably the most boring book of the Old Testament, or, possibly the most interesting. It's a whole book about how exactly God wanted them to worship in the Tabernacle, how to make the offerings, how to pray the prayers. Leviticus does not command God's people to do simply their own thing; they are commanded to worship in specific ways. And after 26 chapters of specific instruction, we get this verse: "I will walk among you and be your God, and you will be my people" (Leviticus 26:12). The "you" is plural. God says God will walk among us when we worship, together.

That's a shocking thing to read about the God of the universe being so present with people that it would be described in a physical way like that: I will walk among you. It reminds me of back in Genesis when we read that God walked in the garden with Adam and Eve.

It reminds me, too, of something in the New Testament.

READ 1 CORINTHIANS 12:7-12, 27

God walked in the garden with Adam and Eve. God walked among the Israelites when they worshiped in the Tabernacle. God walked on earth as Jesus. And now, post-resurrection, we are the body of Christ. The manifestation of the Spirit is in each of us, but none of us has all of it. None of us is the whole body, but only a part. So God walks among us now when we are the body together.

Pastor Francis Chan said in a recent podcast, "If I understand the church biblically, the more of us that gather to pursue him, the more of God we'll experience."[12]

It's great to connect with God individually, but if you're not connecting with God in a worshiping community, you're missing out and we're missing the unique piece of the body of Christ that you are.

Next, spiritual but not religious folks tend to connect with God in nature, and in ordinary events, rather than set times and places. They might say, "I find God in the sunset when I walk on the beach." Or "I see God when I talk to my 3-year-old granddaughter or when I hold hands with my loved one."

The good? Just read the Psalms. There's a long history in our faith of people connecting with God in nature or in the beautiful moments of life. "Let the heavens rejoice, let the earth be glad; let the sea resound, and all that is in it. Let the fields be jubilant, and everything in them; let all the trees of the forest sing for joy" (Psalm 96:11-12). God can surely be found in beautiful sunsets and sweet moments of life. Thank God for those things! We could all do well to look for those beautiful, ordinary moments throughout our week.

The bad? If your entire faith is based on beautiful sunsets, what do you do when a storm comes along? If your faith is found in adorable things said by a child, what do you make of it when that child throws a tantrum and says ugly things instead? Or becomes gravely ill? If your faith is found in your romantic relationship, what do you do when the feelings fade or that person disappoints you?

---

[12] Chan, Francis, "This is the Question Your Church Needs to Ask," https://soundcloud.com/churchleaders/francis-chan-sensing-gods?fbclid=IwAR376mq8n6978an_obju_vSrMc1JCAqqDw193nc_ZokV2hjuHLUl vKBgQSc

Lillian Daniel, a Congregational minister and author, wrote a rather scathing blog post a few years back called "Spiritual but not Religious: Please Stop Boring Me." She writes:

These people always find God in the sunsets. And in walks on the beach. Sometimes I think these people never leave the beach or the mountains, what with all the communing with God they do on hilltops, hiking trails and ... did I mention the beach at sunset yet?

There is nothing challenging about that. What is interesting is doing this work in community, where other people might call you on stuff, or heaven forbid, disagree with you. Where life with God gets rich and provocative is when you dig deeply into a tradition that you did not invent all for yourself.

Can I switch seats now and sit next to someone who has been shaped by a mighty cloud of witnesses instead? Can I spend my time talking to someone brave enough to encounter God in a real human community? Because when this flight gets choppy, that's who I want by my side, holding my hand, saying a prayer and simply putting up with me, just like we try to do in church.[13]

Third, those who consider themselves spiritual but not religious tend to be spiritual tourists, mixing and matching what they like from various traditions. You might hear them say, "I read about Jesus but also the Buddha," or, "I pray to God but I also study Hindu meditation."

The good? Many other religions and belief systems have good in them that we can learn from and be inspired by.

The bad? I don't know about you, but sometimes the spiritual practices I need the most are the ones I like the least. I don't need a religion of my own picking and choosing of just the things I like. That's like the kid who at 10:00 p.m. says they need a latte because they're tired; no, you tell that kid to go to bed. They want a latte, but they need sleep.[14] Left to my own devices, I'd pick the spiritual

---

[13] https://www.huffingtonpost.com/lillian-daniel/spiritual-but-not-religio_b_959216.html
[14] Chan, Francis, *Letters to the Church*, 52

practices I like, the things I prefer, over and over again. I need to be governed by a religion that's not of my own making.

Fourth, spiritual but not religious folks believe that they are avoiding the hypocrisy and the imperfections of the church by not being a part of it. You might hear them say, "Well, church has a lot of things wrong with it. Scandals, corruption, prejudice."

They'll tell you everything from the Crusades to modern history to the pastor they heard of who got in trouble for something, as their reasons for not being a part of organized religion.

Valid point. I know so many people who have been truly, deeply hurt by the human institution of church. If you personally have trouble walking in the door of a church because some church person in your past harmed you, misguided you, made you feel small, let you down… I'm sorry. I hope you'll give church another try. Don't give us another chance to be perfect, because that won't happen. But give us another chance to be an imperfect but loving family of God.

The church I was a part of in high school was a growing, new United Methodist congregation, so we had new members join almost every week. And the pastor would add to the standard membership vows, saying, "You are joining an imperfect church, full of imperfect people, led by an imperfect pastor."

And the people still joined! Because the great thing is, if you're imperfect, too, you'll fit right in. If I avoid church because of its sins, I am left alone with… my own sins. The Bible says, "as iron sharpens iron, so one person sharpens another" (Proverbs 27:17). It says, "confess your sins to one another and pray for each other so that you may live together whole and healed" (James 5:6). As I see it, the greater concern is not that the church is full of hypocrites and sinners, so I'd better stay away. The greater concern is that we're all hypocrites and sinners, me included, and I sure need to be with these other people so that we can challenge each other and grow through our weaknesses.

Finally, those who are spiritual but not religious tend to connect with God on an as-needed basis, or when they authentically feel like it, not by rote, repetition, or expectation.

They might say, "I want to pray or worship when its real and authentic, not just because its expected."

When I was little, when it cost extra money to make a long-distance phone call, we would call our grandparents on Sunday night after 8:00 p.m. They lived in a different state than we did, so we saw them on certain holidays, and for a week in the summer; they sent gifts for birthdays and we sent thank-you notes in return. Those were expectations. Expectations that over time built a relationship. If you were to ask eight-year-old me whether I wanted to chat on the phone with two elderly people who can't hear very well on a spotty phone connection about "what are you learning in school these days?" whether I authentically feel like doing that? No. I want to play My Little Ponies or watch cartoons or swing on my swing set.

But it was an expectation. It was something we did. Week in and week out I had little conversations with them; sometimes a bit stilted, sometimes great. But those conversations built a relationship so that when I got to see them, we weren't total strangers, they knew what I liked to play with and what kind of books I was reading and what my least favorite foods were and I knew what they were up to on their retirement travels and with their neighbors and friends. And over the years, bit by bit, a call or visit or card at a time, our relationship grew and grew.

And now that they're both gone, I'm so glad that my mom made me call my grandparents each week, and I'd do anything to be able to talk to them again.

Our relationship with God works kind of the same way. If we only reach out to God when we feel like it, or only when we need something, that relationship won't be as strong as it could be.

Our Christian tradition gives us a framework, expectations, that are kind of like that weekly phone call. You pray and read Scripture daily. You worship weekly. You serve. You give. Even when you don't feel like it. And over time you build the kind of relationship with God that will feel as close as a beloved family member, all because you did the things that you didn't feel like doing at the time.

Christianity &... Scientology
Romans 5:1-8

This sermon was preached in Clearwater, Florida, the spiritual headquarters of Scientology. The strong presence of Scientology affects our city in many ways. As a result of this sermon, I received positive feedback from many ex-Scientologists who found the sermon via social media and wanted to share their stories with me.

When I first moved here six years ago now, I met a college sorority sister for dinner downtown on my first night here. I saw a bunch of people in uniforms and I assumed they were a bunch of hotel employees all getting out of some sort of convention or training and spilling out onto the streets all at the same time. Later that week I came down Cleveland Street to Ft. Harrison Ave. to make my first hospital visits. And I thought, "Huh, that hotel worker convention still seems to be going on."

Eventually someone clued me in to the fact that our city houses the Flag Service Organization, the spiritual headquarters of Scientology worldwide. So, the beliefs and practices of Scientology are of particular interest to us who live here in this place. As followers of Jesus who live here, it is important that we understand what Scientology is, how it is similar to and different from our Christian faith, and how it operates, so that we can be the hands and feet of Jesus here in our city.

If you were to go to Scientology's own website and click on "What is Scientology?" you would then be taken to a multiple-choice section, asking which of these topics you are the most interested in: how to handle stress, how to have a happy marriage, how to be more successful, how to raise a family well. This gives us a big clue to understanding what Scientology describes itself to be.

Scientology says that it offers a precise path to understanding yourself better as a spiritual being, and thus *improving* every aspect of your life. It claims to bring together the ancient wisdom of older religions with the latest in science and technology. Most of all, it claims to be *practical*; it's not just something you believe, they say; Scientology is something you do that will actually better your life.

Scientology was founded in 1954 by L. Ron Hubbard. He taught that humans are spiritual beings called *thetans*, that humans are essentially good, but that many of our troubles in life come from what he called the reactive part of our mind, which records and stores past traumatic events called engrams. Hubbard taught that the way to clear those engrams is through a process called auditing, which is a little bit like counseling, in which a trained auditor asks you questions to help you locate these painful memories while you are hooked up to an e-meter, which measures electrical changes through your skin (somewhat like how a lie detector works) as you hold onto the handles while talking about these past memories.

When I was in seminary and took a very introductory counseling course, one of the first and simplest methods we were taught was simply to get people talking about painful things in their past, not to solve or give advice, but just to be a safe space for them to talk while we would listen. So we learned to reflect back to them what they've said ("so, what I hear you saying is…"), to validate their experiences ("that makes sense.") and to ask open-ended questions ("tell me more about that.") You can even try these things next time your spouse or child is upset about something instead of advising or arguing or fixing and see if it doesn't do some good. People are starving to be listened to.

You can see why people in Scientology find some benefit from auditing. It works somewhat like this form of counseling. You get to talk about your past pain. You feel heard. No one gives you advice, but the process of sharing eases the burden a bit. So, early on in Scientology people find that it is helping them. So they continue. The goal for Scientologists is to achieve a state called 'clear' in which they are no longer affected by any engrams or their reactive mind.

In addition to auditing, Scientologists are encouraged to take courses studying the teachings of L. Ron Hubbard. Many of the courses early on in Scientology are about practical topics like stress, goals, organization, or communication. I found these all listed as online courses on their website that a beginner could take. These course sound practical and helpful, right?

If you know someone in your neighborhood or workplace who is a Scientologist, this is likely the level of Scientology that they practice. They probably consider it beneficial, not cult-like or dangerous.

The goal of Scientology, though, is to keep going; to progress up the Bridge to Total Freedom. And it is at these higher levels of Scientology where their teachings are closely guarded, not available to non-Scientologists or even to those lower on the bridge. You can find these secret doctrines online or in documentaries by those who have left Scientology; a creation-myth in which spirits from another planet were sent to Earth billions of years ago where they continue to cling to and cause problems for humans. Just as you will find ex-Scientologists who will share these teachings, the church will just as quickly deny that these teachings exist, so we cannot really know for sure.

So how does all of this compare to Christianity?

Scientology says we are spiritual beings who can follow the bridge of L. Ron Hubbard's teachings, courses, and auditing to achieve happiness and success. They believe in some sort of infinity or supreme being, but a personal God is not central to their faith. Nor is sin, salvation, heaven, prayer, or worship.

Christianity says we are spiritual beings who are both created in the image of God and marred by sin. God is central to our Christian faith; we believe in a God who exists in relationship: Father, Son, and Holy Spirit. Christianity says that God wanted a relationship with us so much that he sent his Son to earth to live, die, and rise so that we could be forgiven and rise again after our death to live eternally with God in heaven. Christians believe that this salvation is a gift of grace that we can't earn or deserve, but that we can be transformed over time as we grow in faith through our spiritual practices like prayer, Scripture, worship, and serving.

In a nutshell, Christianity says, we could not make it up a bridge to God. So God came down a bridge to us.

READ ROMANS 5:6-8, 5:1-5

On their own, the beliefs of Scientology that I've outlined may sound strange to you, but not particularly harmful, maybe even helpful to some people. The problems come in how the organization is run, how those beliefs are carried out by the Church of Scientology, particularly after the death of L. Ron Hubbard. These problems are well-documented in our local newspapers, books and documentaries by those who have been inside Scientology and left. They tell of extreme pressure on members to spend more and more money on Scientology services, and pressure not to question or criticize the Church of Scientology. They tell of a policy of disconnection in which Scientology members should cut off family members who are not supportive of the religion. They tell of a strong stance against psychiatric help, which has led to suffering and even death as the Church of Scientology seeks to treat people themselves who actually need medical help. They tell of a fair game policy of attacking those who attack Scientology. They tell of the substandard living conditions for members of the Sea Organization who work for very little pay and believe that they have signed billion-year contracts and cannot leave.

The Church of Scientology would deny all of these things and has many times. But those who have escaped from Scientology tell of these same abuses again and again, and I believe them.

So, what do you, a Christian living in Clearwater, Florida the spiritual hub of Scientology, do in response to this?

We don't need to make fun of them, point at them, treat them like side-show freaks, or avoid walking near them when we see them. Sadly, when I was first getting oriented to life in Clearwater, that is a lot of what I'd hear about Scientologists: mocking or avoidance. These are people who found a belief system that they thought was helpful, and then over the course of years became trapped by its policies; they have spent tremendous amounts of money, they feel they cannot question Scientology, and they can't leave, or they'd risk losing their families. If anything, we can pray for these people and treat them with kindness.

We can support organizations such as The Aftermath Foundation run by ex-Scientologists who are helping those who want to escape and reunite with their families.

We can be wise with our dollars and our votes. Not paranoid or afraid, but wise.

The final thing we can do is to consider all of the things we think are awful about Scientology and choose to do the opposite. We can live a different, better example as Christians.

If you have a child or family member who does not share your Christian faith, there is no reason to cut off relationship with them. We are not a faith that tears families apart.

If you or someone you know has mental health issues, embrace psychiatric help along with prayer. We believe God can work through doctors and counselors. We are not a faith that would ask you to refuse medical help.

If you see someone living in substandard conditions or being abused, that's not in keeping with our faith; help, serve, and work for justice. Our faith tells us, when we do it for the least of these, we have done it for Jesus himself.

If someone wrongs you, our policy is not 'fair game' or 'get even,' our policy is the policy of Jesus to turn the other cheek, to go above and beyond in love.

If you have doubts or concerns about something in Christianity, express them. Ask. Talk. Explore. God is big enough to handle your doubts. We are not a faith that forbids doubt.

What I want you to leave with today is not just information about Scientology or what's wrong with it, but inspiration to love our city, to pray for all the people in our city, and to live your faith in the most Christ-like way possible in the hopes of pointing more people not to a bridge to be climbed up by themselves but to a God who came down to us.

Part 2:
Biblical Exegesis Sermons

Making Sense of Revelation: Hang in There
Revelation 1:1-11

READ REVELATION 1:1-11

When I was a junior in high school in 1998, I got involved with a youth group full of kids who were also very passionate and excited about their faith. Right around this time, a new series of Christian books came out that was very popular. Everyone was talking about them, so of course I started reading them along with all my friends. The series? *Left Behind.* Maybe you read them, too. The series of 16 books and three films were an attempt to bring the book of Revelation to life by exploring how it might play out in modern-day events. True believers in Christ are 'raptured' (taken instantly up to heaven), leaving the world in chaos. Those who remain are left to deal with things like the Antichrist, the 'mark of the beast,' and a seven-year period of tribulation. Being young, impressionable, relatively new Christians, these books caused my friends and me quite a few nightmares and worries about the end of time, which, between these books and all the talk about Y2K, we were pretty sure would be happening any day. "What if the rapture happens before I get to graduate from high school, or, more importantly, before I get to kiss that boy in youth group I've been flirting with?" "What if I'm a true believer but my family's not? How will they withstand being left behind?" "Is the Anti-Christ alive somewhere; is it someone we see and hear about on the news even?"

Needless to say, Y2K came and went. We all graduated from high school. Life carried on. And most of us no longer spend daily time thinking or worrying about the end of days being upon us.

Are those our only two options for understanding this book of the Bible? Option 1, as a coded series of predicted events, that if we can just de-code them, will tell us exactly the who's, what's, when's, where's, and how's of the end of the world. Or, Option 2, something to basically ignore because it's strange and hard to understand, and hasn't happened the way people thought it would so far, so why bother to read this part of Scripture for ourselves?

Might there be something in this book of the Bible that is hugely important, not just for something off in the future, but for our actual lives here and now? Might there be a message in there that would transform our relationship with God and our lives today? I think there is.

If we're going to understand what Revelation has to say to us, we need to know a little bit more about who wrote it and where it came from. Most scholars would agree that Revelation was written around 95 A.D. during the reign of the Roman emperor Domitian. The emperor Domitian was known for persecuting Christians in Asia Minor (which is where Revelation was written to, to the churches in Asia Minor). Christians were required to pay homage to the Roman emperor, calling him "Lord and God." Those who didn't, those who preached about Jesus, those who were seen as troublemakers for practicing their Christian faith, suffered the consequences.

Revelation was written by one such person who got in trouble for his faith. He wrote Revelation from the island of Patmos, which was basically an island for exiling (punishing) people. John tells us that he has been sent to this island because of talking about Jesus in an empire that was hostile to Christian faith. While he's on this island, he is inspired by God to write this message to the churches around Asia Minor. It is addressed to seven specific churches: to the church at Ephesus, to the church in Smyrna, to the church in Laodicea, and so on. Seven is also a number that symbolizes completion (there are days in the week; there are seven orifices in your head), so this was also a way of saying that this letter is being written to the whole, complete church.

The other thing to know is what kind of literature he was writing. If, thousands of years later, someone is examining the ruins of Clearwater, Florida, and they come across the ruins of your house and they find some written materials; it would be important to know if they are reading a love poem or a grocery list, an instruction manual or a novel. The very first verse of Revelation tells us that it is a revelation (hence the name). The word in Greek is "apocalypse."

Revelation is written in a particular literary style that existed in that time called *apocalyptic*. It's a type of literature that is as different from other literature in the Bible (letters, gospels) as my grocery list is from a love letter. Apocalyptic literature occurs other places in the Bible (Daniel Chapters 7-12, for instance) as well as in texts outside of the Bible from about 200 B.C. to about 100 A.D. Apocalyptic literature was usually written during a time when there was widespread suffering and persecution. This type of literature used visions (that were not meant to be chronological or concrete), used wild and weird images and symbols, and even seemed to have a hidden meaning (so that those doing the persecuting would not know what was being written). The message of apocalyptic literature was always this: we are in a present time of suffering, but God is still God. A time is coming when God will intervene, and good will triumph over evil, so hang on! Stay faithful! Don't give up hope!

The best explanation for what apocalyptic literature is like is that it has similarities to a political cartoon. If it were election season and there was a cartoon with, say, a donkey and an elephant… you'd know instantly what that means, right? The two political parties. Democrats and Republicans. But take that cartoon out of our current time and country and context, and people in some other culture would have no idea!

Similarly, there are images that are standard throughout apocalyptic literature that would have made sense to the people reading it at the time. Symbols like beasts were common in apocalyptic texts to represent various nations (and the heads or horns of those beasts represented the rulers). Colors were another standard, as were numbers (three for God, four for the four corners of the earth, 12 for the 12 tribes of Israel, seven for completion).

All of the colors and numbers and animals and strange visions were meant to point toward this same idea: we may be suffering, but God is still God. A time is coming when God will intervene, and good will triumph over evil, so hang on! Stay faithful! Don't give up hope! We see it even in these opening verses, "Grace and peace to you who from him who is, and who was, and who is to come" (Revelation 1:4). God was God before these troubles, and God will outlast the troubles of this present day. "And from Jesus Christ, who is the faithful witness, the firstborn from the dead, the ruler of the kings of the earth" (Revelation 1:5). Meaning, who is really in charge here? The emperor Domitian, or Jesus Christ? The emperor can ask people to bow down and call him Lord all day long, but who is really the Lord? We may be suffering, but God is still God. Good will triumph over evil, so hang on! Stay faithful! Don't give up hope!

A few years ago, when I was going through kind of an emotional time, a friend sent me a song. I downloaded it to my phone and played it on pretty much constant repeat for a few months; hadn't heard it in forever and it came up again this week. I was struck by how similar it is to this theme in Revelation. It's by Andrew Peterson and it's called, "After the Last Tear Falls." It says,

After the last tear falls
After the last secret's told
After the last bullet tears through flesh and bone
After the last child starves
And the last girl walks the boulevard
After the last year that's just too hard
There is love

Each verse goes through more hard things; both personal and global. Then the chorus says this:

And in the end
The end is oceans and oceans
Of love and love again.
We'll see how the tears that have fallen
Were caught in the palms
Of the Giver of love, the Lover of all
And we'll look back on these tears
As old tales
After the last tear falls
There is love

The message of Revelation, I think, is not primarily to get us to decode a bunch of mysterious plans about the future, but to tell people that there *is* a future. There is a future in which God is God. There is a future in which the hard thing in your life, or the hard thing you see going on in the world, does not get the final word. Revelation is not so much about the what's and the when's of the end of time; but about the Who. God is God. God wins. Hang on. Don't give up! Don't lose hope. After the last tear falls, there is love.

Making Sense of Revelation: Sing in the Storm
Revelation 5:1-10

Evan's birthday was last week (he turned three), which obviously led me to think about when he was born. And whenever I think about that, I get pretty mad at him. He was born ten days late. In summer. In Lakeland, the armpit of Florida. I was already off of work, so all there was to do was walk. I walked the Lakeland mall every morning, and the three-mile loop around Lake Hollingsworth in the afternoons. Nothing. And every night the pain would get bad enough that I'd think something was going to happen, and then I'd close my eyes, and then I'd wake up and it would be morning. Still pregnant. So back to the mall and start the process over again. For ten days.

Have you ever been waiting for something? Specifically, waiting for something difficult to be over with? Waiting to get a job after being unemployed? Waiting for chemo treatments to end? Waiting for something to change in a broken relationship that you don't know how to fix? Waiting for a spouse or child to want help for their addiction? Waiting for the grief or the depression or the anxiety to subside a little? Waiting, and crying, in the words of the Psalmist, "How long, oh Lord?"

This is kind of what the people in our Scripture for today were experiencing. We've been talking the last few weeks about Revelation and how the strange symbols and images in this book are not meant to be an exact, detailed, chronological prediction of how and when the world will end; they were meant to give persecuted Christians in 95 A.D. an artistic and inspiring picture that God wins in the end, evil will be defeated, so don't give up hope, and don't stop being faithful.

READ REVELATION 5:1-10

John sees a vision of God on a throne in heaven, and he sees a scroll. The one who is able to open the scroll is Jesus. It turns out, the process of unrolling this scroll is really long; there are seven seals, followed by seven trumpets, followed by seven angels, followed by seven bowls.

With each of these symbols in John's vision, dramatic and terrible events unfold on the earth. Earthquakes and famines and wars and plagues. Each time it seems like one of these cycles is finally about to end, but then another cycle begins. After the last seal, then there are seven trumpets bringing seven more bad things. Then after the last trumpet, there are seven angels bringing seven more bad things! And on and on and on it goes; this actually summarizes Revelation Chapters 5 through about 17; so, a large percentage of the entire book. Can you imagine how John's original readers were feeling as they were reading page after page after page of destruction and turmoil and fear? "How long, oh Lord, must this go on?" Kind of the same about how they might have been feeling about the oppression from Rome. How long? How long. If the book of Revelation is, as some people see it, primarily a detailed schedule of what exactly will happen when the world ends, it's weird, and pretty terrifying. But if it's primarily a picture of hope that encourages people who are suffering to keep their faith in God, because God wins in the end, that's something I need to hear. And I bet you do, too.

First, notice this. Jesus is in the midst of it all. Jesus is standing right there in the center of all of the cycles of destruction unfolding. "Then one of the elders said to me, 'Do not weep! See the Lion of Judah, the Root of David, has triumphed. He is able to open the scroll and its seven seals'" (Revelation 5:5). The Lion of Judah and the Root of David were both Old Testament terms for the kind of Messiah that the Jewish people expected; one who would lead the armies of God's people like a lion; a King, a ruler like David. The emphasis was on raw power.

And then, the next verse, Revelation 5:6, shows us this: "Then I saw a Lamb, looking as if it had been slain, standing in the center of the throne…" Not a lion, but a Lamb! And not even just an ordinary lamb, but one who had been slaughtered. Jesus stands at the center of this long cycle of suffering (the seven seals, and the seven trumpets and all of that) as one who has himself suffered at the hands of a broken world, as one who has himself cried, "Father, take this cup from me." When you or I are asking, "How long, oh, Lord," we are asking someone who has asked it, too. He's been there, too. Our Lord is not a lion, but a lamb who was slain. We are not alone.

And, notice that the slain lamb in this picture is still standing. He wins. Through his suffering, death, and resurrection, he has defeated sin, he has defeated death, he has defeated evil. This book tells us how the story ends. He wins. He does it with a different value system than what the world expects; but he wins. The struggle may go on for longer than we'd like or expect, but we know how the book ends. He wins.

Standing at the center of all the evil and suffering of the world, standing at the center while you ask, "How long, oh Lord?" is Jesus. He has been there. And he has won.

The next part of this text made me think of the Adam Sandler movie *Waterboy*, where Rob Schneider repeatedly says, "you can doooo it."

In Revelation 6:17, after six of the seven seals on the scroll have been opened and a whole bunch of bad stuff has happened, we read "For the great day of wrath has come, and who can stand?"

Who can stand? The question hangs there after six cycles of suffering and destruction. It says that everyone from kings to slaves is hiding and crying out, "who can stand?" Presumably, the answer is, no one. No one can withstand this. Maybe you know the feeling.

And then, the text switches gears, pauses in the cycles of destruction, to answer the question, 'Who can stand?" And the answer is not: no one. The answer is: God's people. "Then I heard the number of those who were sealed, 144,000." Numbers are always significant symbols in this type of literature. Twelve is always the symbol for God's people because there were originally twelve tribes of Israel. Therefore, multiples of twelve, multiplied again by 1,000, would symbolize all God's people, past, present, future. Who can stand in this time of suffering? You might not think you can, but God's people can. You can do it.

And then at the end of this chapter we read:

"Who are these people?"

He said, "These are the ones who have come out of the great tribulation. They have washed their robes in the blood of the Lamb.

Never again will they hunger, never again will they thirst. The sun will not beat upon them; The Lamb at the center of the throne will be their shepherd; he will lead them to springs of living water, and God will wipe away every tear from their eyes" (Revelation 7:14-17).

In the midst of these chapters that seem to be endless cycles of suffering, John stops to answer this question, "Who can withstand it?" God's people can.

How? I've seen you do it, even this very week:

I was making some calls to people who have been sick, and I reached someone on her cell phone who was in the Emergency Room with a family member. I asked, "Do you need me to come over?" "No, three of my friends from church are already here." You can stand; with community.

I've sat this week with people dealing with depression, anxiety, mental illnesses, addictions. And I heard again and again, "I've got a great therapist" or "I'm in a group that's helping me," or "I'm going to meetings," or "I'm in a program to get help." We can stand, maybe not alone, but with the people God gives us to help us.

I went to go celebrate a graveside funeral in which the family only expected three or four people to come; they didn't want to burden anyone in the middle of a work day. I stood there as car after car arrived from this church family, and since the entire choir showed up, we sang. We can stand, with others. You can do it.

I don't know if you've noticed this, but there are numerous songs in this section of Revelation. In Chapter 5 alone, there are three times that God's people burst into song. In the entire section of the cycles of the seals, trumpets, and bowls, there are as many as 27 songs, depending on how you count. It's like an episode of Glee—people are just walking around bursting into song!

Eugene Peterson (who wrote *The Message Bible*) says this in his book on Revelation: "These people are not only secure, they are exuberant. This is a curious, but wholly biblical phenomenon. Throughout

Scripture, God's people sing. They sing in the desert, they sing in the night, they sing in prison, they sing in the storm." [15]

Even as they are crying out, "How long, oh Lord?" they sing. They sing because they know the end of the story. They sing because they know that God wins. They sing because they know that God is bigger than their suffering.

Revelation is not a book that attempts to answer the question, "Why does a good God permit evil and suffering?" That's another message for another day. So much of Revelation is about evil and suffering… but it doesn't really seek to answer "Why?" Evil is not explained but enveloped. It is put in its place. These cycles of suffering, seven seals and seven trumpets and seven angels and seven bowls are overcome by Christ, by worship, by prayer, by the knowledge that God wins. And so we sing in the desert, we sing in the storm, even as we cry, "How long, oh Lord?" we sing.

Peterson gives this example in the same book I mentioned earlier. He says he was teaching this passage of Revelation to a small group, and one of the members of the group asked if she could tell her story. She said that years earlier, she'd had a nervous breakdown. Her whole life was in chaos; nothing fit together. She felt defeated by evil, by guilt, by sheer bad luck. She went to a counselor and he guided her to take a good look at each detail that she had lumped into a large pile and called "evil." Item by item, she looked at each event, each feeling, each problem. Not one of them, she said, became any less horrible. But something else happened while she was doing it. She began to discover other things in her life that had been obscured by the great lump of piled-up wrongs; relationships that were delightful; songs that were beautiful; sights that were heart-stopping. Later, she came to know Jesus, and it all came into focus for her. None of the evil was abolished, but it was all in a defined perspective. The nameless evils had names. The numberless wrongs were numbered. She didn't know when exactly her perspective had shifted, but now it seemed that it was in fact the good that was endless, the glories that were beyond counting. Nothing had changed; and somehow everything had changed.

---

[15] Peterson, Eugene, *Reversed Thunder*, 1988, pg. 62.

The book of Revelation paints a picture of suffering and evil going on way longer than we'd like. And it's not explained. We don't get a good 'why' from this book. What we get is this image that evil is surrounded. It is contained. It will one day cease; and it is, in fact, the good that is endless; the glory that is beyond counting.

And so we sing in the desert, we sing in the storm, even as we cry, "How long, oh Lord?" we can stand, and we can sing.

Praying the Psalms:
The Cursing Psalms
Psalm 109

A couple of people in our household lately have been very into Harry Potter. The books, the movies, eventually the theme park. This has resulted in us pretending to do wizard spells from the Harry Potter stories for ordinary things around the house. Need the TV remote? "Accio remote." Want to open a door? "Alohomora." Need to clean your room? "Scourgify!" Most of the spells in the Harry Potter stories are fun and harmless, but there are a few that are hurtful, some even deadly. So there have been conversations about not putting curses (even pretend ones) on your siblings or classmates or parents.

Strangely, this is the same issue that comes up in our Scripture today in the Psalms. There are 150 Psalms, many of them attributed to King David, but likely written by poets or musicians who worked at the Temple. These Psalms were used as prayers or worship lyrics when people worshiped God. The Psalms were prayed regularly by Jesus and quoted all over the New Testament. They express the whole range of human emotion— from sorrow to joy and everything in between. One particular type of Psalm expresses anger. Not just expresses it, but actually prays for God to harm or even kill the Psalmist's enemies. These are called the cursing Psalms.

- "O God, break the teeth in their mouths" (Psalm 58)
- "May they be blotted out of the book of life" (Psalm 69)
- "May his children be fatherless, and his wife a widow" (Psalm 109)
- "How blessed will be the one who seizes your infants and dashes them against the rocks" (Psalm 137)

These are the equivalent of curses! Praying, urging God to do something bad to your enemies. There are as many as 10 Psalms within the 150 that would be categorized as 'cursing' Psalms ("imprecatory" Psalms). So, a significant portion of this book of the Bible is spent on the author asking God to curse his enemies.

The Psalms were the prayer-book, the hymnal, of God's people, and of Jesus himself. If they're a model for us to use for prayer, can we pray even these cursing Psalms? Are the cursing Psalms trumped by Jesus' words to love our enemies? Or are these prayers somehow helpful tools to us when we are dealing with anger in a relationship in our lives?

Let's take a look at Psalm 109, the most extended of the cursing Psalms, and see what you think.

READ PSALM 109:1-5

This is not just some anonymous enemy. This is personal. This is a friend; someone the author knows well. This person has betrayed him, lied about him, attacked him without cause. Have you ever had something like this happen? It's worse when you're hurt by a friend than by a random stranger, right?

READ PSALM 109:6-15

Now we get into nine verses of cursing. May his days be few. May his children be fatherless. May this bad thing happen, may that bad thing happen. Each one of these "may" lines is like a formula, asking God for these curses to occur.

READ PSALM 109:16-20

Now he's making a case for why this guy deserves this bad stuff.

READ PSALM 109:30-31

The Psalmist ends by thanking God for dealing with this and for saving his life from his enemies.

I asked you before, have you ever been in the position that the psalmist was in? Had a friend or colleague or a family member turn on you? Have you had someone speak badly against you, betray you, lie about you, and you don't feel like you deserve it? Has someone ever done something to you and you've been so angry at them your heart is racing, your muscles are tensing up, your mind starts going a mile a minute with all the things you'd like to say or do to them, you can just feel anger welling up inside of you? The question today is, what do we do with that kind of anger?

Should you run and get your Bible and pray Psalm 109?

Some say no. There's an article in my study Bible right next to this Psalm that says, "If we follow Jesus' example, we dare not mouth the cursing Psalms when we think of our enemies. These Psalms are not for us to borrow from, as are other Psalms."[16]

Some say yes. Dr. Ellen Davis, my Old Testament professor from seminary, tells about a time when she was teaching on the cursing Psalms at her church, and someone questioned her, "surely you don't mean we should pray those!" She writes about this in her book, *Getting Involved with God*, and she replied, "Yes, I do mean to say that Christians should pray these offensive Psalms that call down God's wrath upon our enemies. Or, better, we should know that these Psalms are available and even appropriate for Christian prayer. But, like many good tools, they must be used responsibly, lest they become dangerous to ourselves and to others."[17]

While you certainly wouldn't want to pray these prayers lightly (like if someone cuts you off in traffic), I think there are times where the cursing Psalms can help us to bring our anger to God so that God can transform it. Here's what Psalms like 109 can do for us when we have that kind of anger.

The words of a Psalm like this one put our feelings into words. Having words with which to express our anger can take us from that feeling of blind rage to being able to describe how we feel. Even these terrible cursing words help us to organize our feelings into something that can be named, and in naming it, the anger loses some of its power over us. Words like Psalm 109 also show us we're not the only one who has ever felt this way; we're not the only one who's ever been in such a terrible situation. Seeing our feelings in print like this give us words

---

[16] *The Student Bible*, Phillip Yancey, ed.
[17] Davis, Ellen. *Getting Involved With God*, 2001, pg. 26.

for our anger and show us that there are other people out there who have felt what we feel.

More than just describing our feelings, a Psalm like 109 helps us to bring our anger to God. The cursing Psalms, like other Psalms, are addressed to God. This makes it different than just venting to a friend. When you pray words like Psalm 109, you are bringing your situation to the God of the universe.

When we pray a prayer like Psalm 109, we're asking God to handle it, rather than taking it into our own hands. "No personal vendetta is authorized, no pouring sugar in the gas tank, no picking up a gun or hiring one."[18]   Saying terrible words like these to God is far better than actually acting on them in real life.

When we pray words like Psalm 109, we're giving God power to change us. When we pray these cursing words, we're praying to the one who has the power to destroy your enemies. But we're also praying to the one who has the power to forgive them. The one who even has the power to change your heart. That's a risk to take when you're really, really mad. It would be easier to go out and get revenge. It's a risk to bring your anger in prayer to God, because God might decide to bring forgiveness and healing to both of you instead.

The first time I taught about the cursing Psalms, I was a junior in college, and I was teaching a bunch of youth group kids about prayer. I had them go around to different stations that showed them different ways of praying. I don't remember much of it now, but I do remember the station where they prayed about anger. There were words from Psalms like 109, 137, and other cursing Psalms, and there were a bunch of pillows, in a big, open chapel space. And as students came to the station, they read the instructions, and if they had something, they were angry about, they could scream these words as loud as they wanted. They could punch the piles of pillows as hard as they felt like it. Apparently, middle schoolers have a lot to be angry about. Apparently, I should have probably also warned the pastor and the preschool and other people using the building, because it sounded more like a murder scene than a youth group lesson on prayer!

---

[18] Davis, Ellen, *Getting Involved With God*, 2001, pg. 27.

But one by one, students came out saying that it was helpful to have words for their anger. They appreciated knowing that the God of the universe could handle them praying about real issues in their lives. They liked hearing how there was a community of people going all the way back to Old Testament times who have been mad at a friend (their little 8th grade situation was not the first one ever to happen), and in some cases they could begin to sense God guiding them toward forgiving or healing the situation somehow.

What do we do with anger? Psalms like Psalm 109 show us how to bring it to God. And then, may we, like the Psalmist, end up singing this song of praise: "With my mouth I will greatly extol the Lord; in the great throng of worshipers I will praise him. For he stands at the right hand of the needy, to save their lives from those who would condemn them" (Psalm 109:30-31).

Peter: The Sequel (Acts 4)
Acts 4:1-20

All month long we've been learning about Peter, Jesus' right-hand man. We learned how Peter grew up in fishing towns around the Sea of Galilee and eventually started his own business. How he'd run into Jesus several times before but became a follower after a miraculous catch of fish when Jesus called Peter to become a fisher of people. We saw Peter trust Jesus enough to walk on water, while the other disciples stayed safe in the boat and didn't even try. We saw Peter rightly call Jesus the Son of God, but wrongly reject the idea that Jesus would have to suffer and die. We saw Peter promise to stick with Jesus to the end, only to deny that very night that he even knew him. Then we saw Peter and Jesus re-united after the resurrection by a charcoal fire, and Jesus gave Peter another chance to follow him once again. "Do you love me?" Jesus asked Peter. "Feed my sheep."

That's like the end of Act One of Peter's story. And then the book of Acts is like the sequel. What's Peter going to do with his second chance? Will he deny being a follower of Jesus again the next time things get hard? Will his flaws – his temper, his fear, his impulsive nature— get the best of him? Or has Peter really changed? Is he really ready to follow Jesus and feed his sheep? And if he can, what can we learn from him? Because I think following Jesus and feeding his sheep is something we'd all really like to be able to do.

We'll take a look at one story today, Peter's sequel, the book of Acts, today and see how he does. The reading for today picks up right after Peter and John had healed a guy outside the temple gates and then preached about Jesus to the crowd of onlookers.

READ ACTS 4:1-2

They are healing and preaching right outside the Temple, where people are supposed to be coming in to make their Jewish sacrifices to keep covenant with God. And here are Peter and John, right outside the Temple, doing miracles and preaching this new thing, that Jesus is the Messiah and that he had been raised from the dead. The captain of the Temple guard, and some Sadducees (who are a sub-group within Judaism who did not believe in an after-life or resurrection of the dead) found out about this and they were not thrilled. It would be as if a new religion set up shop out in the church parking lot and was offering free healings and preaching their religion right outside our doors where we're practicing ours.

READ ACTS 4:3-4

They didn't even get to the end of their sermon before they were carted off to jail; and yet five thousand more people believed in Jesus that day. This is concerning for the Jewish and Roman authorities, who probably do not want a mob of five thousand more people who think that Jesus is a higher authority than the Temple or the Empire.

READ ACTS 4:5-20

Peter, who had denied knowing Jesus for fear of arrest, is now willingly getting arrested for his ministry. He is facing the same Sanhedrin Jesus faced. Maybe you recognized the names if you've read the gospels (or seen Jesus Christ Superstar): Annas, the high priest, and Caiaphas. Peter is being questioned by literally the same ones who questioned Jesus on the night that Peter denied him. The fear, the hesitation, the willingness to deny Jesus that had been so present in Peter before, are replaced with courage and confidence.

I read an article this week that called Peter "the patron saint of the tongue-tied."[19] Because he shows us that God can use an uneducated, ordinary fisherman who had made mistakes, doubted, feared, was wrong a time or two, and denied even knowing Jesus three times. If you ever think you're not educated or impressive enough for God to use you, Peter says you're wrong. If you ever think that the mistakes you've made in your past disqualify you from God using you, Peter says you're wrong. If you think that God doesn't want to use you because you've doubted or feared, even if you have turned away from your faith completely at times, Peter says you're wrong. Just because you've chosen fear or doubt in the past, you can choose courage in the

---

[19] http://www.ekklesiaproject.org/blog/2012/04/the-patron-saint-of-the-tongue-tied/

future. God can use you! Just look at Peter, the patron saint of the tongue-tied.

How did Peter become this bold and courageous and transformed? What changed? He tells us. In Verse 20, Peter says, "we cannot help speaking about what we have seen and heard."

What's something that you cannot help talking about? A restaurant, a movie, a concert, a vacation? If you have talked to me in the last month or so, I have probably told you that we saw Paul Simon in concert in Tampa at Amalie Arena. It was one of the very last concerts of his farewell tour, and it was *so* good! He played two encores. He had a 16-piece band. Every musician was incredible. He ended the whole show with "The Sound of Silence" with just him alone on stage. It was so good. I was in Home Depot last weekend and while I was waiting for the employee to help me, a Paul Simon song came on the radio and I said to the employee, "I saw him in concert you know. Last month in Tampa. He played two encores, he ended with The Sound of Silence, it was really good." The guy responded, "Okay... did you need help finding a new dryer?" I am not normally one to chat with strangers in stores, but I just couldn't help talking about this concert.

You've had something like that before, right? Something that you're just so excited, so moved, you cannot help talking about it?

Can you imagine a world where we were that excited, that moved to talk about our faith? Not to tell people about why they're wrong. Not even to argue theology with them. But can you imagine our society if Christians were so moved to tell people what we've experienced with Jesus, here's what he's done for us, what I love about God. Can you imagine a world in which followers of Jesus couldn't help but talk about our faith?

Did you know that in a recent study, over 50% of non-church-goers said that they would attend church if someone they know personally invited them? Fifty percent! That's a lot! The same study also says that only 21% of active churchgoers invite anyone to church in a given year.[20]

---

[20] https://www.christianitytoday.com/pastors/2007/july-online-only/102704.html

So, that means that you and I probably have friends who would go to church if we invited them, who are open to hearing about Christian faith and would like to know more. Fifty percent of our friends would like to hear more. Only 20% of us are saying anything.

But how? But what to say? What if it gets weird? I know. These are all valid concerns that I also share. But let's look at Peter's example. He healed a guy who was in need. Okay, maybe we can't miraculously heal but we can all help. We can all serve. When people saw what he did, they asked, "by whose power did you do this?" In what name? By whose power? And he took that moment and he pointed not to his own power, but to Jesus' power.

We can all do that. Serve. Do good in the world. And take opportunities when they come to point to Jesus and not ourselves.

Here's one difference, though. If the police came over the store intercom in Home Depot and said, "You have to stop talking about the Paul Simon concert" I could absolutely stop. And I would. It was good, but if I were going to get arrested, I could stop talking about it, it wasn't *that* big of a deal. I could even stop talking about seeing Hamilton on Broadway. And CrossFit.

Peter, upon threat of jail, torture, and death, said "I DO NOT CARE, I CANNOT STOP TALKING ABOUT THE LIFE, DEATH, AND RESURRECTION OF JESUS."

I do not say that to make you feel like your commitment to Christ is weak compared to Peter. If you hear this and think, "Wow, I'm not sure I'm that passionate about my faith," you're not alone. I'm not sure I could do what Peter did either.

I tell you about Peter's commitment not to make you feel weak by comparison, but because his commitment proves to me that Peter saw something real. Even when threatened with death, he could not stop proclaiming what he saw. Because it was real. He saw Jesus die; and he saw him alive again. He had that conversation with him by the charcoal fire, he saw holes in Jesus' hands and feet, and Peter knew this death and resurrection thing had really, truly happened.

The dramatic change we see in Peter and the other disciples, the transformation from one who denied Jesus the last time things got tough, to one who will die for him now convinces me they saw something real. They did not change themselves and become stronger, more faithful, and bolder just by trying harder. The resurrection changed them.

And if the resurrection changed them, if it was real enough to change Peter. It can be real enough to change me. And you.

Isaiah: Send Me
Isaiah 6:1-13

There was a series on British television; it's related to the American series "Dirty Jobs," but this one is called *The Worst Jobs in History*. It highlighted the most disgusting or dangerous or tedious jobs, not just in our day and age, but throughout history. Some of the very worst jobs included chimney sweep, executioner, rat-catcher, and, the one I personally found to be most awful, a leech collector. (In the 1800's, they would gather leeches for medicinal purposes, often using their own arms or legs to lure the little critters.)

In our Scripture for today, Isaiah is called by God to take on a terrible job. Maybe not quite as bad as a leech-collector or an executioner, but still, pretty bad. Isaiah is called by God to bring a message of destruction and devastation to Israel. Lots of people are willing to preach about God. But God tells Isaiah from the beginning that this isn't good news he is being called to preach. Isaiah is sent to tell the people that, as a result of their sin, Israel will be destroyed by its enemies. God tells him no one will listen, no one will believe you, everyone will hate you, and eventually they'll probably kill you. And Isaiah still said yes to this terrible job. I wonder why? What would compel him to take on such an awful task?

Today we're going to take a closer look at this story and see if we can find out.

READ ISAIAH 6:1

In the year that King Uzziah died... a significant time in the life of Israel. Imagine the times in your lifetime when a President died while in office. Who remembers when President Kennedy was assassinated? President Roosevelt died in office in 1945; do a few of you remember that? William Harding died of a heart attack in 1923; raise your hand if you remember that one!

King Uzziah had been sick for years with leprosy, and his son had been the king-in-waiting until Uzziah actually died. Enemies such as Assyria were eagerly waiting in the wings, hoping to expand their territory. They were ready to capitalize on any weakness in Israel, such as a lame duck king, or a new young leader just stepping into power.

READ ISAIAH 6:2-4

In this tumultuous time of political uncertainty, Isaiah has a vision. It is of the Temple. Which makes sense, since Isaiah is living in Jerusalem where the Temple is located. He probably worships at the Temple regularly. But this time, in his vision, he actually *sees* God in the temple, on the throne. And God is so big, so majestic, that the hem of God's robe fills the entire temple.

It is as if Isaiah went to the Temple like it was any other day, and the last person he actually expected to see there was God. You know what I mean, right? We come to church. We expect to see our friends; we expect to sing some songs and pray and hear from Scripture but the last thing we actually expect is for God to literally show up in our midst!

But that's what happens in Isaiah's vision. There's God. The hem of his robe filling the whole place. God is so big and the worship that is coming from the angels who surround God is so powerful that the whole place shakes and fills with smoke. It's like an earthquake.

One thing that's unique about the call story of Isaiah is that it doesn't take place at the beginning of the book. This is Isaiah Chapter 6. There are other call stories in the Bible; Jeremiah and other prophets. But they usually are called by God at the beginning of their story. We're six chapters in. I think this earthquake moment represents a change in Isaiah's life. I think God had already been in Isaiah's life; he'd been preaching to people for years. God had been in Isaiah's life, but God was small in Isaiah's life. The kind of faith where God just fits in to your existing beliefs and agendas, where God is there to work for you, not the other way around.

After this earthquake temple vision experience, Isaiah saw that God was bigger than him. And if God is bigger than me, then everything in my life gives way to God. If God is bigger than me, I can't shape him or fit him in or keep him out. If God is bigger than me, then God doesn't work for me; I work for God.

And instantly that causes Isaiah to confess his sin.

READ ISAIAH 6:5

When Isaiah saw how big, how powerful, how holy God really was, he instantly saw himself as small, as unholy, as a sinner. And that might sound negative or depressing, but I'd rather have a faith that tells me I'm not perfect but there is grace, than a faith that tells me I am perfect and don't need grace.

READ ISAIAH 6:6

One of these six-winged angel creatures starts flying at him with a hot coal. He must think he's going to get burned. He's confessed his sin and now God's going to punish him. Burn him. Torture him. Even kill him. This angel is going to zap him dead with this magic hot coal. That's what we think a lot of the time, right? If God really knew me, if God really knew what I'd done, what's in my heart, what's in my mind, God would punish me. Smite me. Strike the building with lightning. Whatever.

READ ISAIAH 6:7

God wasn't punishing him at all. God was purifying him. God was cleansing him, taking away his sin and guilt. It probably hurt, but it wasn't a punishment. Tim Keller is fond of saying that the good news of the gospel is that "We are more sinful and flawed than we realize, and that we are more loved and accepted than we ever dared hope."[21]

But, there's more. Isaiah wasn't just forgiven and cleansed of his sin. Now God has a job for him.

READ ISAIAH 6:8

Literally one second after Isaiah realized that God is holy and that he is a sinner, he is now not only forgiven but called. He doesn't even wait to hear the job description. God says, "Who will go for us? Whom shall I send?" And Isaiah is so transformed by this experience of

---

[21] www.timothykeller.com

realizing that he is both really sinful and really loved by God, that he doesn't even ask what he's being sent to do, he just speaks up immediately: "Here I am, send me!"

And that's how Isaiah got a terrible job. A lot of times when this Scripture is used, the reading ends there, "Here I am, send me!" and then we all sing "Here I Am, Lord" and it ends on a happy note.

But Isaiah's vision doesn't stop there on that happy note. It continues and he finds out exactly how awful this job from God is going to be.

READ ISAIAH 6:9-10

God is saying, the people will never hear you, they'll never listen, they'll never accept you, and they'll always reject you. But it's more than that. God actually tells Isaiah that his job is to close the ears of the people, to close their eyes, to harden their hearts. That is awful, right? Why would God want to harden anyone's heart or close anyone's eyes and ears to God's message?

The few times in the Bible where it talks about God hardening someone's heart – most notably Pharaoh in the Moses story in Exodus—the person has already hardened their own heart many, many, many times. And God, finally, says to the person, "Fine, your will be done." The people Isaiah is dealing with have said for years, "We don't want to hear this! We don't want to hear this message about turning to God and being faithful. We don't want to hear it." And now, finally, God says to them through Isaiah, "You don't want to hear this? Fine, you're not going to hear it."

God is big. God is holy. God is infinitely powerful. But God will not make you follow. God will not make you obey. God will not make you listen. God will not make you love. Because its only really love if you choose it.

So God tells Isaiah to go and preach this terrible message of doom and destruction to Israel. I bet he would've rather been called to be a leech collector! In Verse 11, Isaiah asks, "How long, O Lord?" How long is this going to take?

READ ISAIAH 6:12-13

It's going to take everything. It's going to take complete and utter destruction.

But notice that last phrase in Verse 13. A holy seed will be in the stump. When a forest has burned to the ground, seeds survive and are even activated by the fire, so that eventually new life will emerge. God tells Isaiah, it's going to take total destruction. But it's never hopeless. You're never really alone, never really without God, never really without hope.

It's kind of like Israel as a people is going to have to go through what Isaiah went through as an individual. Realizing the bigness and holiness of God. Realizing his own sinfulness. Having that experience that felt like it was going to destroy, but it turned out that God wanted to cleanse, to forgive, to purify.

Israel will have to find out as a people what Isaiah found out in that vision: that we are far more sinful and flawed than we realize, and, that we are far more loved and accepted than we dared hope.

There's another image in the Bible of God showing up in the temple and causing an earthquake; Matthew 27:50-54:

> *And when Jesus had cried out again in a loud voice, he gave up his spirit. At that moment the curtain of the temple was torn in two from top to bottom. The earth shook, the rocks split and the tombs broke open...When the centurion and those with him who were guarding Jesus saw the earthquake and all that had happened, they were terrified, and exclaimed, "Surely he was the Son of God!"*

Isaiah's vision from so long ago is fully realized in Jesus. God is big and holy and powerful. We are flawed and sinful. We expect punishment but instead God cleanses us, forgives us, purifies us, and then calls us to work for God. Even if the job is hard, may we respond like Isaiah, here I am, send me.

Jesus in the Gospel of Mark: Jesus' Healing Ministry
Mark 2:1-12

Sometime last fall, I had one of those doctor's appointments where they say, "Um, we think we've found something you need to get checked further." It turned out to be a total false alarm. I'm 100% fine. But it was a two-week wait until I could get it checked out, and during that couple of weeks there was a lot of anxiety, a lot of "what if's" and a lot of prayer for healing. Maybe you've been there, too.

Just last Sunday, I heard that Frank, one of our members, was in the hospital and wanted me to come see him. So the boys and I headed over after church to what they call "the hop-sit-al" and visited Frank and prayed with him for God to heal him. The next day I sat with some family members whose loved one was in surgery. The day after that I talked with someone about their struggles with depression. I heard from someone else with trouble in their marriage and prayed with someone else in desperate need of a job. I talked with old friends who are dealing with infertility, and others who are in the throes of hard phases of parenting, and others dealing with busyness and anxiety. Even as I worked on this message at Starbucks, I paused for a moment and listened to the conversations all around me and it was clear that lots of us are in need of some kind of healing in our lives.

Which is why I think the healing stories of Jesus are so compelling, and why the gospel writers spend so much time on them. Jesus casting out demons. Jesus curing lepers. Jesus healing the sick, giving sight to the blind, forgiving sinners, restoring ostracized people to community, even raising the dead. These stories show his power. They show us that Jesus wasn't just some teacher talking about peace and love; he was the Son of God! These healing stories also show Jesus meeting the real needs of real people. Needs like the ones we come with today.

READ MARK 2:1-12

After Jesus was baptized and spent 40 days in the desert, he went back briefly to his hometown of Nazareth. But he found that it's hard for people who knew you in diapers to see you as much of a prophet. So he headed out to the Galilee region and spent most of his ministry in the town of Capernaum. This is the town Simon Peter was from and if you were to go there today, you would see the ruins of a church, built over the top of what was Simon Peter's house, with a glass floor so that you can look down and see this house. They think this was probably where Jesus ate and slept when he was in Capernaum (since he didn't have a house there) and that this is probably the site of quite a few of the miracles we read about in the gospels. Including today's story.

This house is maybe 600 square feet. To get an idea of the size, picture when you walk through Ikea and they have those fake tiny apartments all decorated to show you how you can live fashionably in the world's tiniest space. So it's a super small house. Minus the Ikea décor. And the Scripture says that when everyone heard Jesus was back at his home base, so many gathered that there was no room left, not even outside the door. I picture people crammed into the tiny Ikea apartment, sitting in the windowsills, and crouching up on top of tables, crowds crammed in everywhere, to hear Jesus preach.

There were some people, though, who weren't able to come that night: the sick, the lame, the injured, the depressed, the afraid. You heard how the one paralyzed guy was carried on a mat by four of his friends, and that when they got there and the house was full, they didn't just turn around and go home. They dug a hole through the thatched roof and lowered their buddy down to Jesus. And then Jesus offered the man both forgiveness and healing. He got up from his mat, and he was able to walk. This is one of those great, memorable healing stories: the friends, the mat, the digging down through the roof. These friends were so determined; they would stop at nothing to get their friend to Jesus, the one who they knew could heal him. Jesus said, "because of their faith" (the friends' faith, not the paralytic himself) he would be forgiven and healed.

I wonder, though, about the others, somewhere in the city of Capernaum, who were paralyzed by injury, or illness, or grief, or anxiety. I wonder about all the others who didn't make it out to Simon Peter's house that night to be healed by Jesus… because they didn't have any friends to put them on a mat, carry them over, dig through the roof, and lower them down. Surely there were others in town who couldn't come to Jesus that night because they didn't have those friends with a faith that would stop at nothing to get them to the one who could heal them.

As I studied this story this week, I had a thought. I wonder if the life of faith is supposed to be primarily communal. I wonder if the Christian life is primarily a team sport, rather than an individual one. We live like it's primarily individual. Me and God. I pray. I read my Bible. I sin, or don't, I ask forgiveness, I seek to follow Jesus in my little individual life. And then for an hour a week, we come and do that while all sitting in a room together. We sing some songs. We shake hands. Sometimes a doughnut is involved. We live like it's mostly an individual sport, one that occasionally brings us here to refuel at the same place. But what if the life of faith is primarily communal?

I look at this story and I see where Jesus said that because of *"their* faith," the friends' faith, he will heal this man. It's like there is no rigid dividing line between the friends and the paralytic; they, collectively, had faith. They, collectively, got him to Jesus to be healed. A Catholic woman named Catherine Doherty one said, "Without prayer, the life of the Christian dies."[22] She means, straightforwardly, that if you stop praying, your spiritual self will shrivel up like fruit. But her statement also doesn't specify whose prayer is required to keep your faith from dying. Even when you are so paralyzed by illness or guilt or fear or sadness that you feel unable to pray… if you've got four friends with faith, if you've got people praying for you, if you have stretcher-bearers who will stop at nothing, they will bring you to Jesus when you're not able to bring yourself.

A lot of us are in need of some kind of healing in our lives. What if the answer to that is that we are meant to be stretcher-bearers for one

---

[22] Winner, Lauren, *Still: Notes on a Mid-Faith Crisis*, 2013, pg. 67.

another? What if the answer to that is that the life of faith is primarily communal?

Have you ever noticed that the prayer list at churches (not just ours) is usually a list of those who are sick? Or having surgery. It's almost 100% medical; a litany of our collective illnesses and infections, aches and pains. Almost never does someone publicly ask their church community to pray because they're struggling in their marriage. Or because they're drowning in debt. Or because they're addicted to something. Or because they're dealing with a sin. Or because they're grieving, or lonely, or feeling lost in their faith.

What if the life of faith is primarily communal? Maybe there are things you don't want emailed out to the fifty people on our prayer chain, but do you have four people you could tell? Do you have four friends like the paralytic had? Do you have four people who know what's really, truly going on in your life, people you can all at 2:00 a.m.? And not just nice people but people with faith, people who will stop at nothing to get you to Jesus, the one with the power to heal and to forgive. What if the life of faith is primarily communal? Do you have four stretcher-bearers?

And, are you that stretcher-bearer for somebody else?

I've done some 5K and 10K races, and a couple years back I decided I was ready to move up to a 15K. That's just short of 10 miles. I picked out the Gate River Run in Jacksonville, which is known for being a huge race and a lot of fun. I was in my corral at the starting line with about 10,000 other runners when they explained that there would be two starting guns. One for us regular people, and a special one, five minutes earlier, for those who were attempting to qualify for the Olympics in the 15K distance. Apparently, this race was a qualifier for the Summer Olympics.

You could tell who the Olympic people were right away. Their race number was a special color, and they were wearing official-looking spandex outfits, and were doing warm-ups and talking with coaches and they all looked very athletic and important. Their starting gun went off, and I'm guessing they were halfway through downtown Jacksonville by the time the rest of us got to go. I had a good race, was making good time, enjoying myself, chatting with some of the other slower-pace people who were running near me. It was going really well. And then, we came upon the last mile of the race and saw the Hart Bridge. It's big, it's green, and it's a steep incline. They call it the Green Monster. People were dropping like flies. Walking, stopping, some even sitting down and getting sick. I'm chugging along, slowly, barely—and there we saw the Olympians, standing up at the top of the Hart Bridge. They had long since crossed the finish line, and they came back to cheer us on! One of them looked right at me and started coaching me! He said, "I want you to hold your head up, stand tall, pick up your knees, take shorter steps. Keep running; you're almost there." After running ten miles and qualifying for the Olympics, they came back to stand on a bridge and watch slow amateurs make themselves sick, to cheer us on. To coach us a little. To help us make it when we couldn't do it on our own. Running sure seems like an individual sport, but in that moment, it was primarily communal. Those who could did everything possible to carry those of us who couldn't make it any more.

If you are in need of some kind of healing today, who are your stretcher-bearers? Who are the people of faith who will stop at nothing to bring you to Jesus when you can't get yourself there? If you know who they are, call them. Don't walk alone. It's not an individual sport.

And if you're feeling great today and you're not particularly in need of any kind of healing right now.... You're one of the ones who can walk to Jesus, who has the strength to carry a stretcher and to dig through a roof. Your life of faith isn't an individual sport, either. Someone is looking for you.

The healing we need is found in Jesus.

Getting to him is a team sport.

Part 3:
Sermons Connecting with Children, Youth, and Young Adults

Young Adults: Do You Need Church?
Ephesians 4:1-13

This message was originally for a statewide young adult retreat; I then shared it with our congregation that Sunday morning.

The retreat speaker from Friday night shared how we're all part of God's story, from the beginning of creation, through Christ, through now, until the end of the story when God finally redeems everything. We're a part of the story. And most of us want to be.

The problem is, although we want to be a part of God's story of redemption, we don't always want to be a part of a local church. There are lots of reasons why.

There are countless articles, books, and studies on why people, particularly young adults, are leaving the church and not returning. The church is judgmental. Anti-intellectual and anti-science. Too linked to politics. Hypocritical. You know the list as well as I do. But what about you? If you're not involved in a church right now, why? If you are involved in a church but you can still relate to not feeling welcomed or wanted in church, why?

I'll tell you a time when a church made someone I cared about feel unwelcome and unwanted. It was the summer between college and seminary. I was a summer intern at a church, and I worked with the youth group. I invited a friend who was in high school to attend youth group for the first time. She came to a Wednesday night service, wearing a tank top, as someone in Florida might be likely to do in the summertime. I didn't know it yet because I'd just started working there, but this particular youth group didn't allow tank tops (among a long list of other dress code items). This high school girl had just walked in to a room of 75 teenagers she didn't know, making an attempt to attend a church event for the first time possibly ever. And the first thing she was greeted with was a request to go home and change because we don't allow tank tops at youth group. It's a small thing, and rules are rules, but she felt embarrassed, and ashamed, and like an outsider. Do you think she came back to youth group? No. Do you think that experience will haunt her if ever in her adult life she gets up the courage to walk into a new church again someday? Yeah.

So, whatever it was for you, whether something relatively small like a tank top, or something much bigger, at some point you have probably felt unwelcomed and unwanted in church.

When we feel unwelcomed or unwanted enough in church to get really fed up with it, this is what tends to happen next: we tend to branch ourselves off like two forks diverging in a road. Faith on one side. Community on the other.

A lot of us keep our faith; we haven't turned away from Jesus. But we make our faith entirely personal. Me and God. Maybe you pray, sometimes you might read the Bible or listen to worship music on Spotify. Maybe you even attend church occasionally but you're not in deep authentic relationships with the people there. When church has hurt us, we tend to individualize our faith.

And, then, the other fork in the road is, we tend to find community elsewhere. We turn elsewhere, not church, to meet our need for community. So maybe you join a sorority or fraternity. Maybe you've got a good group of friends from work or school. Maybe you're on a softball team that hangs out after games and talks about life and supports each other. And this isn't a bad thing; good community is good community. My college sorority sisters are still to this day some of the most important people in my life. At this point we are almost 15 years out of college, and we have been through singleness, marriages, divorces, deaths of parents, infertility, raising babies and kids, changing careers, and serious illnesses. Maybe you have that, too, I hope you have that, too.

But it raises the questions, do you need church as long as you have friends? And do you need church as long as you have faith?

Do you need church as long as you have friends? As long as you have good authentic relationships in your life, people you can call on in a crisis, people who love you no matter what, do you specifically need church as long as you have friends?

And do you need church as long as you have faith? As long as you have a personal relationship with Jesus, as long as your ticket to heaven has been punched, as long as you pray and read the Bible and sincerely love God, do you need church as long as you have faith?

I think so. And, I think, the church needs you. I think you are not as complete as you could be without the church; I think your faith can wither without a community to practice it in. I think our spiritual practices can grow lazy without other people to spur us on. I think sometimes our community of well-meaning friends does not give us the right advice, whereas a community of prayer and Scripture and accountability, they won't get it perfect either, but they will get closer. I think being authentic with God and being authentic with others are all tied up together. I think you are not as complete as you could be without a church community. And I think the church is not as complete as it could be without you.

Check this out from Ephesians 4. This is in the New Testament, one of the letters written by Paul to a bunch of early Christians trying to figure out how to follow Jesus. He writes to them:

READ EPHESIANS 4:1-7, 12-13

Maybe I've convinced you, maybe not, but for a minute just go with my premise that you need and want now to be a part of a church community. Now, how to find one?

We are the generation of endless options. We can get Hillsong United or All Sons and Daughters worship music on our Pandora station and we can podcast everyone from Rob Bell to Andy Stanley. We can glimpse into the everyday life of Christian authors like Jen Hatmaker on Snapchat and Facebook and feel like she's our best friend. We can Yelp the best coffee, the best donut, the best anything and our phone will lead us to it. It's awesome. And then we walk into an average church in our neighborhood and the coffee is only 2 ½ stars; they don't even put any decorative foam art on top. The donuts are just regular old Dunkin Donuts. The décor is old and not in an ironic vintage way but just in an old way. And, some of the people are old, too! And the music sounds like it's just a bunch of volunteers because it is, gasp, just a bunch of volunteers. And the pastor of this little 200-

person church on your little street in your little town is not the coolest or most beautiful or funniest or most compelling speaker in the world because not everyone can be one of the best speakers in the world. I'm not suggesting that pastors and church staff shouldn't try. What I am suggesting is that we are a generation of Yelp reviews and endless options, and so when we finally become convinced that we need a church, and we walk into one, it feels…ordinary. Imperfect. And so you church hop and church shop for a while, but you feel like Goldilocks and the three bears: the big church is too big and impersonal, the small one is too small. The cool church is too loud, the traditional one is too stuffy. The conservative one is too strict, the liberal one is too loose, nothing is "just right" and so finally, for a lot of young adults, you just go back to those two diverged roads of personal faith, and secular friendships.

I'm here to tell you, you can, and in fact I would say you should, go and join an ordinary, imperfect church. Because, I hate to say it, but you are probably an ordinary, imperfect person. Go join a totally average, imperfect church, and help to build within it the authentic Christian community that we all need.

You could go join a church like the congregation I serve. Skycrest was started in 1956, grew very large in the 1960's through the 90's, as many traditional denominational churches did, and then declined throughout the 2000's, until it began growing again about five years ago, where today it sits at an average attendance of about 200. It's in an average neighborhood. We have very few staff and I'm the only full-time employee; most of the ministry that is done is done, imperfectly, by volunteers. At first glance, it's a totally unremarkable, average church. But if you look a little deeper, you'll see the kind of community that we read about in Ephesians.

I have friends at my ordinary, imperfect church who are my age, but I also love being in real, authentic community with people who are in their fifties and sixties. They're on the other side of parenting from me, their kids are grown up and out of the house and they're looking toward retirement; the wisdom that I get from having them in my life is invaluable. I am in real authentic community with people in their nineties, who have seen the world change over the course of almost a century. They know that they are nearing the end of their time on earth and so they have a sense of what actually matters in this life.

My ordinary, imperfect church is in community with hungry people; our guests at our community dinner consistently tell us that they could get food elsewhere but we are the place that treats them the best, because we don't make them eat out in the parking lot; we sit down and talk to them, and learn their names. If you are sick and you are a part of Skycrest, you will be cared for and visited. You as a church are empowering younger people to take leadership positions and bring new ideas to the church, and, sure, there are growing pains and it is not always perfect, but we are trying.

It occurred to me one day a while back now, that these people, all ages of them, are legitimately my friends, my community, my church family. I do not feel any different when I am around them than when I am around other family or friends. I don't feel a separation between my "regular life" and my "church life". They just are my church; they are my people. I happen to be the one with the responsibility to speak and lead, but my job within my community is secondary to my place within the community.

If you're visiting today and you're wondering where you can find a church like this, you can find it in an average congregation on an average corner full of average people. What you find will not be perfect. It's not perfect at Skycrest. The coffee is average. The buildings are old. There are things we can't do as well as we would like to. The people aren't perfect; living in community isn't easy. People sometimes say the wrong thing or need some help to see something from a different perspective. It won't be perfect, but you can help build the kind of community we're all looking for.

John Ortberg has a chapter in his book *The Me I Want to Be*, where he talks about authenticity and community. He ends by talking about the old church hymn, "Just as I Am," a song that talks about coming to God without hiding. He says:

A few people in my life allow me to relate to them just as I am, and I cling to them the way a drowning man clings to a raft. If ever there were a true 'just as I am' church, if ever there were a community where everybody could bring all their burdens and brokenness with them without neat and tidy happy endings quite yet, if ever there was a group where everyone was loved and no one pretended—we could not make enough room inside that building.[23]

---

[23] Ortberg, John, *The Me I Want To Be*, 2009, pg. 152.

Faith Like a Child
Luke 18:15-17

READ LUKE 18:15-17

Maybe you picture this story in a serene setting on a hillside somewhere, with Jesus holding little babies and blessing toddlers and hugging children while peaceful music plays in the background and all the children are smiling and well-behaved.

I picture the scene a little more realistically. Parents, remember when you took your kid to sit on Santa's lap for the first time? When you hand a baby or a toddler over to someone who's not their mom or dad, what happens? Waaaaaa!! I picture this story of Jesus and the little children including some crying babies. I picture some toddlers with ketchup stains on their shirts, and a little boy wiping his runny nose on his sleeve. I picture some kids shy around Jesus, others maybe pushing in line to meet him, someone's got a skinned knee, someone else is hungry, others getting distracted and running off to play tag instead, maybe one kid kicks Jesus in the shins just to see what happens. With a bunch of kids coming to meet Jesus, it wouldn't have been a peaceful scene. It would have been a little crazy, loud, and chaotic.

Something that bugs me in children's ministry curriculum is that they'll take any story from the Bible and make it into a little moral lesson. Be good. Listen to your parents. Be nice to your friends. Share your toys. The lesson I had last week for preschool chapel took a bit of a turn in this direction, when it gave the example of Noah's ark as a lesson on patience: Noah waited patiently in the ark during the flood for 100 days! But then a four-year-old asked me "Why did God flood the whole earth?" And I was a little caught off-guard because Noah's ark is actually a story about the sinfulness of human nature and God's faithfulness not to give up on us anyway, and God's covenant never to destroy the earth again but to remain in relationship with humanity that ultimately led God to redeem us through Jesus Christ. But that's a lot for a four-year-old, so you can see why sometimes it's easier to just stick with "this is a lesson about patience." Be patient. Share your toys. Be good.

But is the primary message of the gospel, "Be good?" No. Romans says, "All have sinned and fallen short of the glory of God." The primary message of the gospel is not "Be good," but "Be saved." Be loved. Be forgiven. Trust in Jesus who was good, even when we're not. And then, be transformed, be called, be sent out into the world to live for Jesus. The message of the gospel is not just "Be good."

So—back to our Scripture— when Jesus says that we need to be like children in order to enter the Kingdom of God, he must not mean "be good". He must mean something more than that. What is childlike, *really* like? Not an idealized picture of a meek, humble, sweet perfectly-behaved little child, but what are real characteristics of real children that can teach us what it might mean to have faith like a child?

Some kids are passionate. Passionate about their interest, their hobby, their sport, whatever it is they're into. Liam loves science, aliens, Star Wars, Legos. He wants to be a scientist, chemist, astronaut, or Lego designer when he grows up. Evan loves frogs, and he wants to be a dentist when he grows up. He loves frogs so much that every single week here when Maxine goes through the prayer requests, she finds a prayer card written out from Evan, to pray for frogs. Probably every kid you've known has had interests and passions that are as unique as they are.

So when Jesus tells us to be like children, maybe, in part, he's asking us, to live a passionate life. God created you uniquely. God made the things about you that make you *you*. God has hopes and dreams and purposes for your life. Don't let the world dull you into being just the same as everyone else. God has a mission for your life that is as unique as you are. God has things that can only be accomplished, people who can only be reached, by you. Maybe growing in faith shouldn't feel like a boring, rote, obligatory thing; maybe it should feel like you felt when you were a kid playing with Legos or a kid daydreaming about frogs, where God is helping you discover more about who you were created to be and what you're called to do in this life.

Some kids are inquisitive. We often think that having faith like a child means to be blindly trusting, never doubting. But a lot of kids I know are incredibly inquisitive. Always asking, why, or how, or how do we know? Or, in this day and age, "Give me your phone so I can Google that." Lots of kids love to learn. Maybe, for us adults, having childlike faith doesn't have to mean blind trust with no more doubts or questions. Maybe it means just the opposite. Maybe it means God wants us to use our brains and bring our questions and doubts to God. To explore our questions about faith in conversation with each other. To learn from people who see things differently than we do. To find that that inquisitive spark inside of us actually draws us closer to God.

Some kids are imaginative. They live in a world that's in-between the real, everyday world, and a fantasy world of imagination. They make sock puppets or pet rocks or talk to their stuffed animals just as easily as they interact in what adults would call the real world. Kids can see a world of possibilities that adults can't. There is a story that I've seen re-printed in several places in which a three-year-old sibling desperately wants to be left alone with his newborn baby sister. The parents think this sounds strange at best, dangerous as worst, so they put it off as long as possible. Finally, they agree to let the little boy go in to his sister's room alone while she's in her crib, but not to pick her up. And the parents overhear him asking, "Baby? What is God like? I'm getting older so I'm starting to forget." Maybe faith like a child is holding onto a bit of that sense that there is a world beyond just what we see, that there is a spiritual realm. That there is more than just what we can see and understand and Google. Trusting that its possible, even when we can't quite understand it.

Some kids have a great sense of fairness. They know what it is to earn a cookie, or to earn a punishment. Kids know what fairness is. They also know what grace is. Every kid knows a time when they should've gotten punished for something and they got forgiven instead. Every kid I know has also done something at some time that was more kind than the other person deserved. Maybe they forgave their sibling, or they were kind to a kid at school who isn't very nice, or they let a younger kid win a race even though the younger kid didn't really win. Kids know about fairness and they know about grace. Maybe having faith like a child means to accept that we are sinners, we are imperfect, we have broken God's laws, and yet God has made this amazing way through Jesus Christ for us to be forgiven anyway.

Some kids are adventurous. One thing I know about kids is that they hate being bored. They want to play. They want to do. They want to have fun. They'll either whine about it, or they'll go out and find something to do, but they aren't likely to just sit around being bored. Kids are adventurous and active and fun. Maybe Jesus had that in mind, too, when he told us to enter the kingdom of God like children. Maybe he meant for us to enter a relationship with God expecting that God has an exciting life in store for us. That God has a calling and a purpose for us that we never would have dreamed up for ourselves. That following God will be exciting, maybe dangerous, maybe challenging at times; but not boring.

When Jesus told the adults to enter the kingdom of God like children, I don't think he meant meek, blindly trusting, or even well-behaved. I think he meant for us to be inspired by children's sense of passion, inquisitiveness, imagination, fairness, kindness, and adventure. That's what I want the adults to hear today.

Here's what I want the kids to hear today about faith. Adults don't always get faith right. Adults can get so easily distracted by adult stuff and adult problems. That's why Jesus said that you, kids, are an example for adults to look to.

So be a great example. This is a great time in your life to have a relationship with God. Having a relationship with God doesn't mean that you have to be perfect. God knows we mess up sometimes and those are called sins. But our sins can be forgiven because Jesus died on a cross and paid a price, took a punishment for all of our sins for everybody. God isn't mad at us. We are forgiven and loved.

You can spend time with God just like you spend time with a parent or a friend. Since you can't see God, it's a little different. But you can read more about what God is like in the Bible. You can learn more about God at church. And you can talk to God out loud, or in your mind, or in writing anytime you want, about anything that is on your mind. That's called praying. God is always with you; God is always listening. Sometimes you might even feel like God is answering you back; maybe not with words, but maybe with a little feeling or an idea of what the right thing to do might be.

Kids, God made each one of you special. God gave you your talents and interests and your personality and God thinks you are awesome. God gave you those talents and interests and personality because when God wants to accomplish something on earth, God tends to use people for those missions. God has plans and adventures for you that are going to be incredible.

So do be good. I think you'll find it's a better way to live.

But even more than that, be forgiven by Jesus. Be loved by God. Be passionate, inquisitive, adventurous, and brave. Just like you are.

Part 4:
Preaching Theological Topics

Why Did Jesus Have to Die?
Romans 5:6-11

Louis Pasteur, a French scientist in the 1800's, and his colleagues were working on a cure for diphtheria, which had been killing thousands of babies and children in their day. They were working on this theory of germs and vaccinations, but at least to this point, no one had believed them. Yet.

They set up a laboratory in a forest and began to monitor the progress of twenty horses who had been infected with diphtheria. Shortly after getting the disease, every horse except one developed a terrible fever and died. Most of the doctors and scientists figured the experiment was pretty much over and did not remain for what they thought would be the death of the remaining horse.

For several more days this final horse lingered, lying pathetically on the ground. While Pasteur was sleeping on a cot in the stable, the orderly on duty had been instructed to awaken him should there be any change in the animal's temperature during the night.

About 2:00 a.m., the temperature showed a half degree decrease, and the orderly awakened Pasteur. By morning the thermometer had dropped two more degrees. By night the fever was entirely gone, and the horse was able to stand, eat, and drink.

And so they took blood from the veins of this animal that had developed the disease but had overcome it. The scientists drove as fast as they could to the hospital in Paris. They forced their way past the guards and went into the ward where three hundred babies lay, segregated to die from diphtheria. With blood of the horse, they inoculated every one of the babies. All but three lived and recovered completely.

They were saved by the blood of an overcomer.

I heard this story sitting in church a long time ago in an Easter service while visiting family in Charleston, South Carolina, and the sermon ended there. We are saved by the blood of Jesus, the one who has overcome sin and death and rose again. We are saved by his blood. The crowd seemed pleased and we stood to sing the closing hymn, "Nothing but The Blood of Jesus," and I remember thinking, "Okay, but how? Is no one else here wondering *how* the blood of some guy who died two thousand years ago has any effect on me?"

Let's see how the Apostle Paul addressed that as we read our text for today:

ROMANS 5:6-11

So why did Jesus have to die? Different Christians over time have looked at the Bible and found a few different ways of explaining this. We're going to talk about three different images today of what Jesus' death does for us. If you were sitting in a theology class somewhere, these would be called "theories of atonement" (there are more than three, but this covers the major ones). This is one of the few things that various groups of Christians don't get too worked up arguing over! Each one of these pictures shed light on a different aspect of Jesus' death. You can listen to these three images and you don't have to pick just one. You can find helpful things in all of them that help you to understand more about why Jesus had to die.

First image: Jesus on the cross is standing in our place. Jesus is our substitute. In the substitutionary theory of atonement, the problem is that we have broken God's laws, and there is a penalty for that. Death, eternal separation from God, is the penalty. The solution is that Jesus pays that penalty for us, as a substitute, taking our place and dying on the cross. "The wages of sin is death," the Bible says in Romans 6:23, "but the gift of God is eternal life through Jesus Christ our Lord."

If you're a really good person, how many times a day would you say that you sin? Would you say three times a day is a good estimate? Three times a day when you are unkind, or untruthful, or don't put God first, or don't love your neighbor as yourself?

Imagine that you're in court, and God is the judge. If you had three violations per day, over the course of a lifetime you've racked up 50,000 sins. And that's just if you're a good person; the number is higher if you're not that good! If we heard of a judge who let someone with 50,000 traffic tickets go unpunished, we'd be outraged. Sweeping that under the rug just doesn't seem right, fair, or honorable. The substitutionary picture of atonement takes seriously that there is a cost to our sin. The penalty is infinitely high. And yet Jesus says he will bear the cost himself. Jesus comes along and takes the consequence of our sin for us. He gets what we deserved, and in turn we get what he deserved, which is eternal life with God.

Second image: Jesus as our example to follow. This would be called the "moral exemplar" theory of atonement. In this theory, the problem is that most human beings are fueled by our own self-interest. Most of the time, I'm pretty focused on me. The solution is that Jesus' whole life and death are a demonstration of selflessness and love; the more we get to know Jesus, the more his example teaches us to live like him. Philippians 2:3-8 says, "Do nothing out of selfish ambition… but let the same mind be in you that was in Christ Jesus, who being in very nature God, didn't consider equality with God something to be grasped… but instead took on the nature of a servant… even unto death on a cross." We are at-one with God because Jesus shows us how to be human. Jesus had to die because we needed to see how to live. He shows us firsthand what selfless love looks like.

Third image: Jesus as the victor. This is the "Christus Victor" theory of atonement. In this picture, the problem is that we are captives, to Satan, to sin, or to a broken human nature. It's like Paul says in Romans 7:19 (The Message) "I try to do good but then I don't do it, I try not to do wrong, but then I do it anyway." Sin is a struggle that is deeper than just some bad behavior. It's like the whole human race was being held captive, and then, the solution, Jesus, came along. He became one of us, joining us in our captivity, died (which is the end result of our captivity). Then he rose again, once and for all victorious over sin and death, and we get to share in that victory with him.

There are stories in our culture that echo this story. In the Hunger Games when Katniss volunteers as tribute, she willingly enters into the broken system. And then she wins! Or Harry Potter at the end has to die to defeat Lord Voldemort, but then he comes back! And the movie theatre erupts in cheers. Perhaps because we recognize this story that evil does not have the last word, that someone has entered into brokenness, and emerged victorious. Jesus had to die because we were enslaved to sin and death. We are at-one with God because Jesus won and set us free.

We have three pictures of why Jesus died. In his life, Jesus is our example of how to be truly human. In his death, God takes on the cost of our sin. In his resurrection, Jesus is victorious over all that enslaved humanity.

Now for the next question, how do we access what Jesus did for us? What does it take to become a Christian? Nothing, and everything.

Nothing, in that all you have to do is accept this gift and it's yours. The Bible says, "confess with your mouth and believe in your heart that Jesus is Lord, and you'll be saved" (Romans 10:9). The guy next to Jesus on the cross, a criminal, simply said, "Jesus, have mercy on me, a sinner," and Jesus told him, "Today you will be with me in paradise" (Luke 23:43). He didn't do anything to earn it; he was a criminal on his deathbed. It costs nothing. It is a gift that is free. You can't earn it. You can only accept it.

But, in a way, it also requires everything. Our whole lives. Because Jesus says that he wants to live in you. He wants to be not just Savior, but Lord.

There is a story about a man who says to the owner of a beautiful pearl, "I want this pearl. How much is it?"

"Well, a very large amount," said the seller of the pearl.

"How much? Do you think I could buy it?"

"Oh, of course," said the seller, "everyone can buy it."

"Well, didn't you say it was very expensive? How much is it?"

"It's everything you have," the seller said.

The man thinks about it for a minute, makes up his mind, and says, "all right, I'll buy it."

"What do you have," the seller wants to know. "Let's write it down."

"Well," the man said, "I've got ten thousand dollars in the bank."

"Good, ten thousand dollars. What else?"

"That's all. I don't have anything else. Well, maybe I've got a few bills here in my pocket. Five, ten, twenty, and some change."

"That's fine. What else do you have?"

"Nothing. That's all."

"Well, where do you live?" the seller asked.

"In my house. Oh, yes, I have a house, but…"

"The house, too, then." The seller writes it down.

"You mean I have to live in my camper?" the guy asked.

"You have a camper? That, too."

"But I'll have to sleep in my car!"

"You have a car?"

"Yes, two, of them."

"Both cars. Those, too. Anything else?"

"This is nuts. You already have my money, my house, my cars, my camper. That's all I have."

"Are you alone in the world?"

"No, of course not, I have a wife and children and a job and friends and hobbies and a whole life…"

"Them, too. All of it." He writes it down.

Suddenly the seller exclaims, "Oh, there's just one more thing. You, too. You yourself. That's what this pearl costs."

When people in the Bible ask Jesus things like "What must I do to be saved?" or "How do I get into the kingdom of Heaven?" Jesus says it's free. But he also says it costs everything, in that you have to stop trusting in yourself, your accomplishments, and being in control. To the rich man who was trusting in money, Jesus told him to sell everything and give it to the poor. To Nicodemus the Pharisee who was trusting in his religious rule-following, Jesus told him to be born again. This gift of new life is free, but it costs you your life; you have to give up control and put your trust instead in Jesus.

I did that in 1997, driving in my car, after hearing this explained at youth group. This moment wasn't the start; God had been working in my life before this through my parents, my church, my friends. Methodists call this prevenient grace. And this wasn't the end; I am far from being a finished product, and I certainly wasn't one at 16 years old. Methodists call that sanctifying grace. That moment wasn't everything, but it was important. (And Methodists call that moment justifying grace.)

If you've never had a moment like that where you have consciously prayed to accept Jesus' gift of salvation, we're going to give you an opportunity now. If for no other reason so that you don't end up doing it in a car later and getting in a wreck!

You can pray along with me silently if you want to.

Jesus, I believe that you died to reconcile us to God. Thank you for doing for me what I couldn't have done for myself. I trust you for eternal life, and I trust you to lead me in this life as well. I want you to be not only Savior, but Lord. Amen.

Zoom: Denomination (LGBTQIA+ Inclusion in The United Methodist Church)
1 Corinthians 13:12-13

This sermon was preached as part of a five-week series exploring what God might want to say to the world, the denomination, our congregation, our families, and us individually. I considered this message the most important one of the series, six months before The United Methodist Church would have its called session of General Conference on the topic of LGBTQIA+ inclusion.

If you've seen The United Methodist Church in national news headlines recently, it has probably been about some kind of controversy or struggle. "Gay minister faces possible de-frocking because he married a man." "Will views on same-sex marriage split one of America's largest Protestant religions?" "1800 Methodists launch WCA to promote conservative values in UMC." "UMC elects first openly gay bishop, in defiance of church rules." "Methodist high court rejects first openly gay bishop's consecration."

Around here at Skycrest, the news sounds pretty different. You may hear that one of our members is having her 100th birthday party, or that Vacation Bible School is coming soon!

You may (or may not) know that we have gay members, gay leaders, and members who have a gay, lesbian, or transgender family member. And that we have church members whose views on this issue span a broad spectrum of opinions. And we all exist pretty well as one church together. I don't preach about this issue every Sunday, or even every year, but I've heard from a growing number of people who want to know:

What is going on with The United Methodist Church? What does The UMC believe about homosexuality, and what if I don't agree? What are these big decisions coming up in 2019, and how will this affect us as a local church?

We're going to talk frankly about this, and I'm going to do my best to preach plainly what I believe God has to say to us. But to do that, you're going to need some context about how we got here as a denomination. So stay with me for the next five minutes as we cover 250 years of Methodist history.

Methodism began with a guy named John Wesley, who was a priest in the Church of England in the 1700's. He was not trying to start a new denomination; he was only trying to make the Church of England better. He emphasized preaching where the people are; he preached in coal mines and fields, which was considered scandalous. He emphasized serving people in need; building schools, orphanages, ministering in prisons and hospitals. He emphasized growing in your faith in small groups. And more than anything else he emphasized grace, the love of God that we don't deserve but is there for us anyway.

Some of Wesley's Methodists came over to America to spread these teachings; but when the American Revolution started, many of them went back home. So Wesley sent two leaders, Coke and Asbury, to America and they formed a new denomination, the Methodist (Episcopal) Church, so that they could do ministry in the colonies, separate from the Church of England.

See, the Methodist Church was founded not out of a theological argument over doctrines, but out of a desire to do ministry with new people in new places. Methodist core beliefs today are really the same as they were in John Wesley's time: grace, growing in faith in groups, and serving the world. At Skycrest we call this "connecting to God, each other, and the world."

Since those early days, The United Methodist Church has become one of the world's largest denominations, with 12 million members worldwide. The UMC is still growing in some parts of the world, particularly in Africa. But it is declining in other parts of the world, particularly in the United States, at a rate of about 70,000 members per year. That will be important to remember in a few moments.

With 12 million people all around the world, we need some organization, some rules. And that's where things get complicated.

The United Methodist Church is organized a bit like the U.S. government. There's a kind of executive branch, bishops. There's a judicial branch, the Judicial Council. And there is a legislative branch, delegates who make the laws of our church. They do this at our General Conference, which is a worldwide gathering that meets every four years, and the rules they make get written into the Book of Discipline.

One of those interesting rules is that the buildings that churches meet in are not really owned by that congregation; they are held in trust and owned by The United Methodist Church. So that means that a local church can't just get mad about one of the rules in this book and say that they don't want to be Methodist anymore.

Starting in the 1970's, rules were proposed and passed into our Book of Discipline that say that "self-avowed, practicing homosexuals are not to be ordained as ministers in the United Methodist Church"[24], and that "ceremonies that celebrate homosexual unions shall not be conducted by our ministers or conducted in our churches."[25]

Our legislators also passed rules into our Book of Discipline that state, "all persons are of sacred worth"[26] and "homosexual persons no less than heterosexual persons need the ministry of the church and deserve to have their human and civil rights ensured." "We affirm that God's grace is available to all persons; we commit ourselves to be in ministry with all persons. We implore our members not to reject their gay and lesbian members and friends."[27]

Remember the part I said about The UMC growing in places like Africa and declining in places like the United States? Our delegates to General Conference are proportional based on membership. So as the United States is growing more accepting of gay and lesbian persons and many in the States would like to change the church's rules to allow gay ordination and gay marriage, more and more delegates are coming from parts of the world like Africa that tend to be more conservative

---

[24] United Methodist Book of Discipline, 2016, paragraph 304.3
[25] United Methodist Book of Discipline, 2016, paragraph 341.6
[26] United Methodist Book of Discipline, 2016, paragraph 4
[27] United Methodist Book of Discipline, 2016, Social Principles

on this issue, and they would like more accountability for those who are breaking the rules. This has led to an impasse every four years at our General Conference on this topic since the early 2000's. I was one of the delegates to General Conference in 2012 and I can tell you firsthand, it felt like we were on the brink of schism; it felt like the entire ten-day conference was a fight about this issue in which no one was listening, nothing was getting done, and everyone was frustrated and hurt. On my way into the doors of the conference, I walked by both Westboro Baptist protestors (who felt we were too open minded on this issue) and gay and lesbian Methodists holding signs explaining how they desperately want to be married or ordained in their church. The talk of a split was constant.

In 2016, our leaders wisely said enough is enough. They said, we need to formulate a Commission, a diverse group of our very best leaders, to come up with *A Way Forward*, whether that be splitting up or figuring out how to stay together. That Commission has met for the last 18 months. They have come up with a plan, and a special General Conference will vote on their plan in 2019. The main plan they are proposing is essentially to allow every local church and pastor to decide for themselves who to marry, and letting every Annual Conference decide for themselves who to ordain. Some people on both sides feel it doesn't go far enough, but many others feel it is a reasonable way forward to keep The United Methodist Church together. There are other plans being proposed and considered, so anything (or nothing) still may happen in 2019.

So that brings you up to speed on Methodism from the 1700's to today! Now for a joke break before we continue. How many Methodists does it take to change a light bulb? Twenty-two. One to climb the ladder, one to hold the ladder. Ten to formulate a committee to evaluate the effectiveness of the old light bulb, and ten to plan a pot-luck to welcome in the new light bulb.

Next, we will take a look at Scripture. What does God have to say to us about homosexuality, and about the future of our church? This is primarily an issue about how we read and interpret the Bible, right? So it makes sense to figure this issue out well as a church because this will not be the last time, we disagree on how to interpret the Bible.

There are six passages in the Bible that specifically mention same-sex relationships.

- Genesis 19:1-29 and Judges 19- the story of the town of Sodom, in which men from that town assaulted two men who were messengers from God.

- Leviticus 18:22 and 20:13, that say homosexuality is an "abomination" come from the section of the Old Testament known as the Holiness Code, which contains other laws like kosher food laws.

- 1 Corinthians 6:9-10 mentions "homosexual offenders" (though some translations say "male prostitutes" or "sodomites") along with drunkards and the greedy and says that they will not inherit the kingdom of God.

- Romans 1:23-27, in which Paul talks about those who exchange 'natural' relations for 'unnatural' ones

Traditionalists on this issue would say that these are in the Bible, and so they are God's word for us today. They believe these passages reveal to us that homosexuality is not God's will, and that it is a sin to be overcome, not something to be affirmed, accepted, or celebrated.

Progressives on this issue would say that these six passages reflect the culture of the time in which they were written, and do not represent God's timeless will for us today. Similar to passages like, "Do not wear clothing woven of two kinds of fabric" (Leviticus 19:19) or "women must cover their heads in church" (1 Corinthians 11:5). They believe that at least some of these passages were about homosexual practice in worship of pagan idols, or in instances of assault or prostitution, not about loving, committed relationships between two equal partners. These persons believe that Jesus' words and example of loving all people speak louder than the six verses about this topic.

And that is where I fall on this issue. I truly believe, after studying these texts in their original languages, knowing the history, studying the commentaries, that the six passages that mention homosexuality reflect the issues and culture of the time and do not reflect God's will toward gay and lesbian persons today.

People I know who are gay, lesbian, or transgender tell me that they knew this about themselves from a young age. They didn't choose this, in fact many of them were afraid they'd be rejected by their family or their church and so they prayed tirelessly that God would change them. And yet God did not. I simply cannot imagine that the God that I know, the God who has revealed himself to us in Jesus, would hold something against people that they did not choose and cannot change.

If a gay or lesbian friend asks me what I believe about homosexuality, I tell them that I believe God loves them, I believe this is a part of who they are, not a sin that they've chosen to commit, and that I believe the best thing *anyone* can do is spend your life getting to know God better, following Jesus, and connecting with other Christians in a church.

READ 1 CORINTHIANS 13:12-13

This can be a hard topic to understand; we see in a mirror dimly. But the next verse reminds us that our task is not just to understand. Our task is faith, hope…and love. Sometimes I ask myself, "what's the worst that happens if I'm wrong?" If I'm wrong on homosexuality, the worst that happens is that I've just invited a bunch of gay people to get to know God better and become followers of Christ. I think I'm okay with that! When it's a hard issue and I feel like I'm seeing in a mirror dimly, I am choosing to err on the side of the thing we were founded on, grace, God's undeserved love for all people. I choose to err on the side of grace.

So that's me. The question for you is, what do you believe about these Scriptures? And can you live together in a church with people who may see it differently? You already are, no matter which side you're on. I think the Bible has a lot to say about diversity and unity in the church. "One body, many parts" (1 Corinthians 12:12). "Make every effort to keep the unity of the Spirit through the bond of peace" (Ephesians 4:3). Jesus prayed in John 17, "that they all may be one."

As for what will happen in our denomination, and at Skycrest? First, this General Conference will vote on this proposal in February of 2019. If it passes, it would be rolled out in 2020. Most everything about our church would stay the same. We will worship, the gospel will be preached, we will grow in faith, and we will serve the world. Gay and straight, progressive and conservative people are already and have always been welcome in our church, in our ministries, as volunteers. The one new thing that may happen is that if a gay couple asks for a wedding here, I would decide whether to do that wedding, and our church leaders would decide whether to allow it on our property.

If this proposal in 2019 does not pass, there may eventually be a split in the Methodist denomination. But I think the greater risk is decline and death. I think the greater risk than a schism is that we spend so long fighting about this that we become increasingly irrelevant to a world that is uninterested in our debates and just needs the true purpose of the church. John Wesley expressed a similar fear back in 1786:

I am not afraid that the people called Methodists should ever cease to exist either in Europe or America. But I am afraid lest they should only exist as a dead sect, having the form of religion without the power. And this undoubtedly will be the case unless they hold fast both the doctrine, spirit, and discipline with which they first set out.[28]

And so I invite you to consider, what do you believe about these difficult passages of the Bible and how to interpret them? Can you live in a church with people who see it differently? And when in doubt, can we as Methodists go back to the roots on which we were founded… growth in faith… service to the world… and the grace of God. When in doubt, can we as Christians go back to these words from our Bible:

"Faith, hope, and love remain, but the greatest of these is love."

---

[28] Wesley, John, *Thoughts Upon Methodism*, 1786.

Part 4:
Sermons for Holidays and Liturgical Seasons

Christmas Eve:
Let Every Heart Prepare Him Room
Revelation 3:20

When I began the sermon, I brought a large, wooden door onto the stage and propped it up in front of the pulpit. I preached next to it and knocked loudly on the door when the sermon called for it. I rarely use props or visual aids, but this one was effective.

There is an image in Scripture of Jesus standing at the door of each one of our hearts, knocking, wanting to come in, but not forcing his way, knocking to firmly yet gently remind us of his presence, but leaving the choice to us to welcome him inside.

I imagine Jesus standing at the door of my heart. Knocking. (Knock, knock.)

"Just a minute!" I call to him. "Hang on a sec! I'm busy."

I've got one kid home sick, a baby in my arms, work on the laptop, dinner in the oven, and a million things on my mind.

"Just hold on a minute and I'll be right there."

While he waits, I wonder if Jesus remembered the stories his mom told him about the night he was born. (Knock, knock).

"Just a minute," the innkeeper had called out to Mary and Joseph, after hearing their knock on the front door of his inn. The innkeeper was probably very busy that night, rushing around, dealing with the multitude of guests who had already checked in, what with it being the census and all. Everyone had to go back to the town their family was from to be registered in the emperor Caesar Augustus' great census. So the usually sleepy little shepherding town of Bethlehem was rather overrun with out of town visitors, many of them staying at the inn. In addition to a busy time at work the innkeeper had his own family, probably a wife and children and animals and extended family to look after.

"Hang on a sec," the innkeeper called out to Mary and Joseph. "I'm busy. Just a minute, I'll be right there."

Back to the door of my heart, Jesus has been waiting more than a minute. And so he knocks again (knock, knock). I answer in a rush, like you might answer your door when there's a well-meaning teenager selling magazines for the class fundraiser or an earnest window washer wanting you to hire him. "Aw, that's nice, I'd like to, but now's not a good time."

Jesus doesn't seem to pick up on my desire to make this conversation quick. He wants to come in! It seems like he wants to come in and hang out for an undetermined amount of time, maybe forever. That seems like a lot.

So I tell him, "Hey, Jesus, here's the thing, there's really no room in here. It's super crowded. There are so many other things already taking up room in my heart, good things like friends and family and hobbies, and maybe some not-so-good things like money and stuff and outward appearances and other people's expectations and worry and pressure and things I'm holding onto from the past. I've meant to clean things out but haven't gotten to it yet. Sorry, Jesus, maybe we can meet up from time to time, but there's just no room for you to come in and stay."

Jesus' thoughts turn again to the night of his birth, the stories his parents told him about the rather unusual way he came into the world. In a cave out back behind the inn, a place meant for animals, because there had been no room for his mom and dad at the inn that night.

(Knock, knock, knock.)

"No room" the innkeeper said. Mary and Joseph had arrived so late, on account of them coming from quite a distance, and Mary being so very pregnant. The rooms were full, and maybe the innkeeper was kind of glad they were. This was a bit of a scandal, word of it may have traveled back to Bethlehem. Joseph and his girlfriend, poor couple, pregnant before marriage, and they're claiming the baby is somehow from God?

"No room," the innkeeper said again. "If you're really stuck without a place you can sleep out back where the animals are. But there's no room in here."

Knock, knock. Jesus, again, at the door of my heart. He's persistent, but not annoying. It's like he knows there's more to the story.

"You could make some room," he says, "If you wanted to. I don't need much space or anything fancy, I just want to come in."

Well, Jesus, the truth is, it's kind of a mess in here, in this heart. It doesn't seem like it's good enough for you. It's kind of shabby, ordinary, messy, for the Savior of the World to come in. There's doubt. There's temptation. There's anger. There's sin. Maybe give me some time to clean things up a bit, and we'll see if we can do this another day?

"Don't you know?" Jesus says. "I left a throne in heaven to be born in a stable. I was the king of the universe and I became a helpless baby, born to a poor couple, in a nowhere town. I spent my first night on earth in a feeding trough. That's why one of the names I am called is Immanuel, God with us. So that there would be no such thing as a heart that's not good enough for me to come into."

So slow down. Make a little space. But most of all just open the door.

(Knock, knock, knock.)

Ash Wednesday:
What God Can Do with Dust
Isaiah 58:1-9

Several years ago, we had a couple different friends staying with us for different reasons. Long story short, we had four adults and a baby living in one house. And one of the biggest things I noticed about having extra houseguests was how much dust there was on the furniture and the wood floors. All of the time! It's gross, but they say that dust is just dead skin cells, so it makes sense: the more people, the more skin cells, the more dust.

Dust and ash are used pretty interchangeably in the Scriptures as a symbol of mourning, or lament, or repentance. Dust is just dead stuff. Dead skin or dead plant matter. Ash is just burned-up stuff. So ancient people would wear sackcloth and put dust or ashes on their heads when they were grieving, but also as a way of saying to God that they are sorry for their sins. Dust is also so fragile, so temporary, it would remind the people of their own impermanence, that they are not God and that someday they, too, will be dead stuff. All of us will someday become the dust of the earth.

People back in Isaiah's day were doing rituals with dust, sackcloth, and fasting. Really similar to what we Christians are doing here tonight. They fasted (they didn't just give up one thing, they were fasting from all food!), they sat in sackcloth and ashes, and were sorry for their sins. They repented, they prayed, they desperately wanted to hear a message from God or feel closer to God, and they heard… nothing. They felt…nothing. Have you ever felt that way?

"Day after day they seek me out," God says in Isaiah 58:2, "They seem eager to know my ways…They ask me for just decisions and seem eager for God to come near to them."

"Why have we fasted," the people say in Verse 3, "and you (God) have not seen it? Why have we humbled ourselves, and you have not noticed?"

God's about to tell them why, through the prophet Isaiah. You're exploiting your workers. You're fighting and hurting each other. People are hungry. People are homeless and in need right in front of you.

And then in Verse 5, God asks, "Is this the kind of fast I have chosen? Is it only for bowing one's head like a reed, and for lying on sackcloth and ashes? Is that what you call a fast, a day acceptable to the Lord?"

God continues in Verse 6: "Is not this the kind of fasting I have chosen, to loose the chains of injustice, to set the oppressed free. Is it not to share your food with the hungry and to provide the poor wanderer with shelter, when you see the naked to clothe him?"

In Verses 8 and 9, God says, "*Then* your light will break forth like the dawn, your healing will appear, *then* you will call, and the Lord will answer, *then* you will cry for help and he will say here I am."

The people in Isaiah's day had forgotten something that I think we forget, too. They forgot something that we, too, forget when we come here to confess and repent and pray. They forgot what we forget—that God doesn't just want dust. God wants to do something with dust. God doesn't just want you to sit around and realize that you're human and a sinner. God then wants to do something with your repentance, your humility, your denying yourself.

Think back to the dust for a minute. From dust you came and to dust you shall return. That comes from the creation story in Genesis, which tells us that God created the first humans out of the dust of the earth. God scooped up this dirt, this stuff of lifelessness, and breathed life into this lifeless stuff, made something out of this sad, dirty, ashy, death-y stuff. God is in the business of doing something with dust. God uses dust to make new life! We see it in Genesis. And then Isaiah tells us, God wants to do something with our dust.

So as we repent of our sins, God wants us in our humility to notice the needs around us. As we use this season of Lent to draw closer to God, God also wants to send us out to others. As we fast to discipline ourselves, God also wants us to give to people in need.

So how might this work in real life today?

I know a lot of you have thought about giving up something for Lent: sweets or soda or something like that. What if we thought about giving up a meal—not just to diet, not even just to fast prayerfully—to be able to buy a meal for someone in need. What if we would give up clothes shopping or social media or whatever you waste time on, not just to pray more, but also to go spend that time volunteering at one of our local ministries in the community. Giving up the $10 a week I spend on Starbucks is not just good for my wallet or a nice thing to do for Lent. $10 a week at Starbucks could buy six bed nets for people to fight malaria in Africa, which is the mission project we'll be supporting as a church this Lenten season.

Malaria was eliminated in the United States in the 1950's but continues to kill a person in Africa every two minutes. It is transmitted by mosquitoes (which feed at night), enters the bloodstream and the liver, and, left untreated, leads to organ failure. Ninety percent of malaria victims are children under five and pregnant women.[29] Malaria is totally preventable with education and treatment. Malaria has already been reduced by over half since the United Methodist Church and other global partners started raising awareness and funds.

Fasting is a spiritual practice that draws me closer to God as I think about my sin and need for grace. But this Scripture reminds us that fasting, in a very real way, creates ten dollars I didn't have before, and that's another bed net I can send to Africa through Imagine No Malaria.

When you come up and hear these words, remember that you are dust and to dust you shall return… those are words of sorrow and also words of possibility. God is in the business of making new life out of dust! God wants to do something with your dust.

---

[29] http://www.umc.org/topics/imagine-no-malaria

Easter Sunday: Believing the Resurrection
Matthew 28:1-10

READ MATTHEW 28:1-10

I heard a story of a dad who was driving around one Sunday afternoon with his little five-year-old son. And they went by a cemetery where there was this big pile of dirt and a freshly dug grave. And as they passed by, his little son with great excitement in his voice, pointed and said, "Look, Dad! One got out!"

The truth is, I think if you're five, it's a whole lot easier, to believe it would be even possible for someone to stand up out of a grave and walk away. But that's what Christians say we believe happened, to Jesus, that first Easter morning.

Do you ever struggle to believe that it really happened? Do you ever wonder? Or, if not, do you ever wonder what to say to a friend or relative, maybe your child even, who wonders whether the resurrection is real.

My eight-year-old son Liam loves to research things. In particular, he loves researching what are called cryptids. Cryptozoology is the study of creatures whose existence has yet to be, or else cannot entirely be, proven or disproven by science. Creatures like Bigfoot, the Loch Ness Monster, Chupacabra, those are all cryptids. In his research, he has learned a lot about proof versus evidence, about how myths sometimes spread from a glimmer of truth, and about how sometimes people are suspected of covering up the truth for their own best interests. Liam has a scale of believability for the things he believes in the most strongly, and the ones he doubts are real.

You probably have a scale like that in your own mind, too, not just for Bigfoot, but for lots of things. UFO's. Stonehenge. Who shot

President Kennedy? There are probably some things that, while they cannot be proven, you believe. And others, you don't.

What about the resurrection? Where does Jesus rising from the dead fall on your own personal believability scale? If you would say it's a little bit hard to believe; check the story, you're not alone! Most of the disciples, at first, didn't believe. Belief did not just come naturally to them right away. If you were to read the Easter story in all four gospels, you'd see a lot of doubt, questioning, and fear. If you doubt or wonder sometimes, you are in good company.

People ask me all the time whether I actually believe in the literal resurrection of Jesus, or whether I think that part of the story was just some kind of metaphor or myth.

I believe the resurrection of Jesus actually happened. Here are some reasons why:

First, the empty tomb. If it wasn't empty, the Roman and Jewish authorities could have simply proven that the resurrection didn't happen. Right? Just produce the body. They could've brought out the body and instantly discredited the whole resurrection. If it was stolen, which seems nearly impossible, they could've found it. With the entire leadership of the Roman empire and the Jewish Sanhedrin wanting to put an end to this Jesus business, I'm pretty sure they could've found a stolen body if there was one to find.

Next, the women, Mary Magdalene and the other Mary. In all four gospels, women are the first witnesses there at the empty tomb.

In that ancient culture, women were not believed reliable enough to testify; in fact, their testimony in a court of law would not count.

And so, if the early Christians writing down the gospels were going to make up a fake story about the resurrection of Jesus, they would have put men, important men, in the story as the earliest ones at the empty tomb. A story that contains unflattering or unhelpful details to your case, is typically not a story that was made up. The only reason to tell it the way that we just read it… is because that's the way it actually happened.

The final thing that convinces me that the resurrection of Jesus actually happened is the dramatic way that the friends and followers of Jesus were transformed by the experience of what they saw that first Easter. When Jesus had been arrested, and on trial, and being tortured and killed, all of Jesus' friends turned away. Denied they even knew him. Were scared to be seen with him or associated with him. It was a dangerous thing to be a follower of Jesus in those early days where they were supposed to claim the emperor Caesar as Lord. And so everyone ran away scared.

But after the resurrection, after that first Easter, we see the disciples fearless, bold, committed, confident of their faith in Christ, willing to go to the ends of the earth preaching about this resurrection, even willing to die for their faith. Many of the original disciples of Jesus, the same ones who had run away scared during his arrest, were now willing to give their lives for the gospel. These people were so transformed from fear to faith; the only thing I can think of that would have convinced them to change so drastically, is that they actually saw the resurrected Jesus, and that their testimonies, recorded for us in the Bible, are true. So, yes, I believe the resurrection of Jesus actually happened.

I also believe resurrection will happen for us at our death. Because Jesus died and came back to life in a new, resurrected way, I believe I will be raised after I die, too. I believe that. When I die, whenever that may be, and breathe my last breath, I believe I that I will awake to a new, resurrected life on the other side of death.

So I'm good with believing in the resurrection of the past (Jesus), and the resurrection of the future (when I die). But what is hardest, I think, for us to actually believe—and here's the point today— is that resurrection is also a present reality in our everyday lives.

 "Therefore, if anyone is in Christ, the new creation has come: The old has gone, the new is here!" (2 Corinthians 2:17)

"I have been crucified with Christ and I no longer live, but Christ lives in me. The life I now live in the body, I live by faith in the Son of God, who loved me and gave himself for me" (Galatians 2:20).

"Since, then, you have been raised with Christ, set your hearts on things above, where Christ is, seated at the right hand of God. Set your minds on things above, not on earthly things. For you died, and your life is now hidden with Christ in God" (Colossians 3:1-3).

I have been raised with Christ. I am a new creation. My life is now hidden with Christ. Christ lives in me! Present tense. Not just past tense. Not just future tense. Resurrection is a present reality. I am resurrected!

Is that really true? I don't always feel resurrected. I don't look resurrected. The Lord knows, and everyone I know will confirm, I certainly don't act resurrected.

What does it mean for me, and for you, in our everyday lives to live as resurrected people, alive in Christ, in our homes, our jobs, our families, our world?

Every time dead stuff in our lives comes to life, we ARE resurrected. Every time a sin is confessed and forgiven, resurrection. Every time someone decides to get help for some habit or hang-up. Every time that someone's heart that has been turned away from God turns toward God, resurrection. Every time a broken, dead relationship takes a step toward healing, resurrection. Every time that hopelessness gives way to hope or purposelessness gives way to calling, resurrection is a present-tense reality.

And it's not just individuals who are resurrected; its communities, too. When relationships are built across lines that usually divide people. When people in need of material things are helped by people who may have plenty of material things but need the spiritual. When people pray together or confess to each other or do life together in community.

Once a month, we serve a free meal for anyone in our neighborhood who is hungry. Over time we get to know these people and their stories, and they become a part of our Skycrest family. Last Easter, the Saturday of the outreach dinner fell on the same day as our Easter egg hunt. I remember a bunch of children were here early before the dinner because their parents were volunteering in the kitchen. So we sent them to go make cards for each one of our dinner guests and put them out at each place setting. Happy Easter. God loves you. Enjoy your dinner. Except kids get their D's and B's backwards so it said, "Gob loves you, enjoy your Binner."

The moms and dads were running around cooking and serving the meal and I saw one of their beautiful little daughters still in her fancy Easter dress from the egg hunt that morning. She ran up eagerly to give her card to an old man experiencing homelessness. No fear. No sense that this person was any different or "less-than" than her. Happy Easter, God loves you, enjoy your dinner. That was resurrection, here and now, in that moment.

Do you believe resurrection happened all those years ago? I do. Do you believe it will happen for you when you take your final breath? I do.

Do you believe resurrection can happen present-tense, here and now, in your life? I believe it can.

Part 6:
Preaching Personally

Service of Death and Resurrection: Glenn Savage
Isaiah 40:28-31

When you first arrive as the pastor at a church, you have funerals for folks you've never met. Which is hard. For the next couple years as pastor of a church, you mainly have funerals for those who have been homebound for as long as you've known them. Still hard. I've been here six years now and pretty much all the funerals I do now are for my friends. People I know and love.

Over the last six years, I've made many visits to Glenn and Mary's home, which is actually more like a beautifully curated museum, full of antiques and collectibles that Glenn and Mary gathered during their work with estate sales over the years: china plates and bird figurines and cigar memorabilia and nutcrackers.

Beautiful mementos of a time gone by.

I wonder if some of those antiques reminded Glenn of the time, he grew up in. He was born in Illinois in 1923 and grew up there with his brothers. He served in the Marines in World War II, got married, started a family, and eventually moved down to Florida in 1974 where he worked for and eventually retired from Montgomery Ward.

Glenn's daughter Gayle was reminiscing about those days, and she said Glenn was the kind of person "for whom nothing was too big." That stuck with me all week; nothing was too big, there was nothing he couldn't do. He was a carpenter and a craftsman. He would take on projects around the home and make sure they were done to perfection. He would use his spare time to help friends or neighbors or church members. A neighbor once remarked that they'd see Glenn in the backyard working and he never walked anywhere, he ran. Doing, fixing, serving, running. Nothing too big.

After Glenn's first wife passed away, he reconnected with a neighborhood friend, Mary, whose husband had also died. The two couples had been extremely close, Mary even helping host the funeral reception for Glenn's first wife. It seemed a natural thing, then, when their friendship, over time, turned to love and they were married here in this sanctuary in 1999.

Glenn and Mary continued to be active in their neighborhood, and doing estate sales, and collecting antiques, and caring for their dogs that Glenn loved so very much. It is a testament to the friendships they built in their community that several of these last times I've been visiting Glenn and Mary, a neighbor has dropped by, or a neighbor was bringing over dinner, or a neighbor was helping with their housework. In a day where we are less connected than ever, Glenn and Mary seemed to have the secret to lasting friendships and community.

Glenn was active, too, here at the church, where they sat over there in their pew each Sunday and were part of the Foundry Sunday School class. Glenn would help out each year at the church rummage sale by testing each electrical appliance to make sure it worked before we put it out for sale. As his health has declined these past few years, we would find someone else to do the job, but we always think of Glenn and how, even later in life he was always doing, fixing, serving. Nothing too big for him.

Glenn's health had not been so good these past few years, but he fought so hard. He struggled with unexplained tremors that took over his body with a violent shaking. And eventually, kidney cancer. He was in a lot of pain, weakness, falling, and generally not feeling good. And yet when I'd visit him, I would leave feeling encouraged; he would use what words he could muster despite the pain to ask about the church or my family or say something positive. Glenn's greatest wish was to live out his days at home, not in a hospital or a nursing home. When he reached a point where he could not do it all, fix it all, where there was in fact something too big for him, Mary and Gayle stepped up and in Glenn-like fashion did what needed to be done to ensure that he would spend his final days in familiar surroundings with the people he loved.

The reality of life is that, finally, all of us will eventually face something that is too big for us. It may be illness. It may be grief. It may be something different for each of us. And when we reach the end of what we can handle on our own, God is there for us.

READ ISAIAH 40:28-31.

There is only one for whom nothing is too big. Jesus. Glenn is with him now. No more tremors. No more pain or sickness or weakness. Glenn and Jesus are probably trading carpentry stories and I bet when Glenn needs to get somewhere in heaven, he runs once again.

And for those of us who remain, when you grieve, trust in the one for whom nothing is too big. When you're lonely, trust in the one for whom nothing is too big. When you're lost, trust in the one for whom nothing is too big.

Your Move: Lead
1 Corinthians 12:1-30

This sermon was preached as part of a summer series focused on the role of the laity in the church. I included it in this section because in it, I share examples of church members using their gifts for ministry.

When I was in middle school, I was on the track and field team. We lived in a small town, so finding people for a girls' middle school track and field team was kind of slim pickings. I liked to run long distance, but because we were short on people, each one of us had to do three events, including one "field" event like shotput, javelin, or high jump. I distinctly remember learning for the first time, through that experience, that there are things we like, there are things we are good at, and things that we are needed to do for the good of the whole. And that sometimes those things match up and sometimes they don't.

I loved running the longest distance available in any race. I liked it. And I was good at it, it was my natural gift.

I wanted so badly to do the pole vault, because it looked cool and fun, but I never could get the hang of it. In fact, I was so bad at it that I was banned from even trying the pole vault because they didn't want to have to take me to the hospital after I missed the soft mat and landed somewhere out on the track instead.

I was just okay at the long jump, but I thought it was boring and uncool. But the coach said that's where I was needed. I did the long jump for the good of the whole team.

I still think of this experience when I think of how God decided that the primary way, he would reach the world would be through local churches, and that the local church would function kind of like a team. There are so many different ministries and things that the church is called to do. So many different kinds of people coming together with different gifts. Sometimes there's things you've just got to do for the good of the whole: taking out the trash, auditing the financial statements. But by and large, the church works best when as many of us as possible are doing our best event, the thing that gets us excited, serving within our gift.

There's some stuff I'm called to do as the pastor. Primarily, that is to preach, administer the sacraments of baptism and communion, and lead the church. But there's a whole bunch of stuff that you, the church, are called and gifted to do.

Have you ever wondered what your gifts are? Maybe you know what you're good at in a work setting but you're not sure how that translates to church. Have you been stuck in a volunteer role that doesn't give you any joy? Have you wanted to start a ministry or try a new idea or lead something but you're afraid? We've probably all wondered at times what our gifts are and how we should be using them.

Let's take a look at our Scripture. This is from 1 Corinthians, which is one of the letters in the Bible written by Paul to a church that he had ministered to and then moved on from. He wrote several letters back and forth with the Corinthian church, and in this part of the letter he is giving them some advice about spiritual gifts.

READ 1 CORINTHIANS 12:1, 4-7

Can you remember a time in your life when God used you and your gifts to accomplish something? It's exciting, right? The first time I can vividly remember being used by God was in youth group; I was a senior in high school and they asked if any seniors wanted to serve as mentors for the new little 6th graders going through Confirmation (a class in which young people study the Christian faith and decide to accept it for themselves.) I led a small group of girls who were going through that Confirmation process, answered their questions about faith as best I could, and on that night when they were confirmed, and actually one of them chose not to get confirmed. I knew that I had helped them to understand what it meant to follow Jesus and really decide for themselves whether they wanted to do it. Realizing that you have a gift and using it for God's purposes is a really cool feeling!

This series is not really because I want something from you, like to join the finance committee or teach Sunday School or do some little chores around the church. This series is because I want something for you; I want you to see for yourselves that there is just no greater feeling, no greater excitement, no greater life-giving joy-producing experience than being used by God to make a difference in the local church which is the hope of the world.

So back to the Corinthians. Paul goes on and talks to them a bit more about what some of the spiritual gifts in that community might be. There are other places in the Bible where possible spiritual gifts are listed, so this is not an exhaustive set-in-stone list, but here are some options for some of the gifts God has given to people.

READ 1 CORINTHIANS 12:8-11, 28

First, apostleship. In the Bible, sometimes followers of Jesus were called disciples, which means learners. Other times, they were called apostles, which means those who are sent. Paul says here that some people are wired with the gift of apostleship. People with this gift get excited when they are pioneering new ministries, they like starting cool new stuff for God. I think of Dave Blakeslee who was a quiet guy who sat in church with his wife and kids; he told me one Sunday he wanted to talk to me about something. We met later that week and he started talking about struggling families in the Skycrest neighborhood, and in the preschool. He asked whether I'd seen all the homeless people over by our basketball courts, and along Gulf-to-Bay and in Crest Lake Park. He said he wanted to feed them a nice dinner, where they sit down and get to talk and feel valued and eat incredible food. Every last Saturday of the month since January, Dave and Staci and their team have done just that, with as many as 60-75 guests on a given night. And it came from that gift of apostleship, the ability to see something that doesn't exist yet, and get it started for the benefit of God's purposes.

Most apostles are not great at all the details and behind-the-scenes stuff. So God gave some other people in churches the gift of helping. The gift of helping has been defined as being able to attach spiritual value to any task that moves God's church ahead. If your gift is helping, you can be peeling potatoes and know that you are doing important ministry. If your gift is helping, you get excited and find joy in working behind the scenes, whether that's taking out the trash or folding bulletins or holding fussy babies in the nursery. If your gift is helping, you find spiritual value in doing whatever is needed. This gift doesn't get noticed as often because it's not usually the person on stage or the one leading the meeting or getting credit for the awesome new idea but helping is a beautiful gift and its one every church needs. I think of the week a couple years ago where we had some unexpected folks resign from our Child Development Center and on that first day that we were short-staffed Jo-Ann Ramsey showed up with Subway sandwiches and ice cream bars for the teachers because she knew they wouldn't be getting a lunch break. A bunch of you worked the food program for those weeks, doing the shopping, making lunches, wiping up spilled milk, not because your gift was food service but because your gift was helping.

Some people have the gift of teaching. Teaching is the ability to get insight from Scripture and explain it in a compelling way. This is something different than being an educator in your profession; you don't have to be a trained professional teacher to have the spiritual gift of teaching. You might have the gift of teaching if you hear or read something in the Bible and your mind starts running with how this applies to people's lives, how to explain it, how to get people excited about it, how to say it to a certain age level. If your mind works that way, you might have the gift of teaching. Ron Read is very soft-spoken and quiet, but 40 or more people sometimes pile into his Sunday School class because he is an incredible teacher. Carla came to me a year or so ago with this idea for a study of Theology and the Arts, and she taught Scripture through movies and music and monologues in a way that changed people's lives. As we grow as a church, we need more of you with the gift of teaching to let us know and find ways to put that gift to use.

Some people have the gift of administration. This is actually my primary gift, and I always hated it. Because it sounds so boring. Administration is the gift of getting stuff done, making stuff happen, seeing the grand vision and then seeing all the little details that have to happen to get us there.

Some people have the gift of creative communication. When people read this passage of Scripture, of course we all notice the spiritual gift of speaking in tongues and interpreting tongues, because it sounds so strange and foreign to us today. It seems that, back in biblical times,

God sometimes gave people the gift of speaking in an unknown language and gave others the gift of interpreting that unknown language, as a way of transcending typical words to communicate a deeper spiritual truth. I believe God still sometimes gives people this gift in this way today; I know people who speak in tongues. Try as I did when I was younger, I never did, it was like the spiritual version of pole vaulting, it just wasn't my gift. That seems to be a rare gift today; what we see a bit more is that God gives people gifts to transcend language through music, through art, through creative talents. I think of Good Friday here, Barb McQuain came up with this interactive prayer station idea that took people through the final events of Jesus' life; it was beautiful and moving and everyone said it was the highlight of their Easter and I had to keep telling them, I had nothing to do with that one. That was someone with a gift for creative communication.

Some people have the gift of generosity. There are some people who are gifted with the ability to earn money, manage and save their money, and then joyfully give whole bunches of it away to advance God's kingdom through the church. Marvin, who came to our Modern service, worked in local businesses right here in Clearwater for most of his life, he wasn't born a millionaire or anything easy like that; he just worked hard, and didn't live outside his means. When he passed away earlier this year from pancreatic cancer, I got a copy of his will because he left a very generous gift to Skycrest to help us do some much-needed renovations to our property. Marvin had always been out volunteering at our work days and he knew that we've got buckled carpet and old wallpaper and air conditioners that break down and he wanted our church to be here for the next generation. And, it gets even better; next on his will was a $30,000 gift to a waitress at Farmer Boy. His will said, quote, "because she was my favorite waitress." I can just imagine Marvin sitting in his financial advisor's office with that gift of generosity that God gave him, with a big smile on his face as he made those plans. People like Marvin have this gift to earn and manage and save money and then to joyfully invest it in the work of God.

The gifts we've talked about today are just some of the gifts highlighted in the New Testament. Go back and read the whole chapter for more and be thinking about which one or ones might fit you.

This section of this letter from Paul also highlights some problems that can come with spiritual gifts.

Those with on-stage, up-front gifts run the risk of arrogance, of thinking they are more important than the others. "The eye cannot say to the hand, 'I don't need you!' And the head cannot say to the feet, 'I don't need you!'" On the contrary, those parts of the body that seem to be weaker are indispensable" (1 Corinthians 12:21-22).

Those with behind-the-scenes gifts can feel like their gift is unimportant, unimpressive, and they wish to be something else. "If the whole body were an eye, where would the sense of hearing be? If the whole body were an ear, where would the sense of smell be? But in fact God has placed the parts in the body, every one of them, just as he wanted them to be. If they were all one part, where would the body be? As it is, there are many parts, but one body" (1 Corinthians 12:17-20).

The final potential problem that can come with spiritual gifts is when we forget that they are from God and for the purpose of building God's kingdom through the church. 'Now to each one the manifestation of the Spirit is given for the common good" (1 Corinthians 12:7). How often have we had a gift, a natural ability, for leadership, teaching, generosity, or administration, and used it primarily to build our kingdom, our career, our net worth, our own interests?

The good news is, it's never too late. It is never too late to discover your gift, and to start using it to serve the one who gave it to you.

Service of Death and Resurrection: Art Brundage
Psalm 84

On my first day here at Skycrest, I got a list of people in hospitals, rehab, nursing homes, assisted living facilities, and the like. Because the list happened to be given to me in alphabetical order, the very first ones on my list were Art and Dorothy Brundage. I entered the address for "The Oaks" in my GPS, and off I went.

The very first thing Art did was tease me, which instantly made me like him more. When I explained that I was the new pastor at Skycrest, he acted like he hadn't heard me correctly, asking, "What? You're a member of the youth group?" This became his regular greeting for me during many of my visits over the next few weeks.

As I got to know Sandy and the rest of the family, as we knew that today would eventually come, she talked to me about some of Art's favorite hymns and Scriptures, which I'd then sometimes discuss with him. One that the family shared with me that I want to share with you today is this:

READ PSALM 84

This Psalm was originally written about the joy of making a pilgrimage to the Temple in Jerusalem. The Temple was the special place of God's presence for the Jewish people; it had layers where different people were allowed, for different reasons, to draw closer and closer to the center, where they believed God's presence dwelled. The court of the Gentiles, the court for Jewish women, the court for Jewish men, the inner court for priests, and then, behind the curtain, where only one High Priest could even go once a year, the holiest place of all where they believed God dwelt.

So this Psalm expresses the joy in being in God's house: "How lovely is your dwelling place! My soul longs, indeed it faints, for the courts of the Lord. Happy are those who are in your house, singing your praise. One day in your courts is better than thousands elsewhere. I would rather be a doorkeeper in the house of the Lord than be anywhere else."

As I got to know Art over these past couple months, and as I've heard stories from his family and friends, I see a man who lived his life, happy to be a doorkeeper in the house of the Lord. Happy to serve others. Offer hospitality. Do whatever he could to keep the doors—doors of churches, doors of opportunity, doors of his own home—open so that all people might be able to enter God's presence. Art lived his life, in so many ways, as a doorkeeper of the Lord; not the kind of doorkeeper who seeks to keep people out, but the kind who seeks to open the door of God's grace wider and wider, to point the way for more people to find their way in. And now Art himself has entered those doors, after 100 years, and has heard those words, "Well done, good and faithful servant."

Art was born June 2nd, 1913, in Peckville, Pennsylvania. He attended Penn State, and eventually worked at IBM in Endicott, New York for over thirty years. He married Dorothy, and together they raised four children—Bruce, Reed, Janet, and Sandy.

Ever a doorkeeper in so many ways, Sandy remembers Art plowing the snow-filled driveways for sick and elderly neighbors, so they could, literally, get out their doors. He and Dorothy were very involved at First Presbyterian Church there in Endicott, where Art served as what would be the Presbyterian equivalent of our Methodist chair of trustees, overseeing the facilities. He was the one on call for emergencies, for custodial work when the church was short on help, and for big projects like removing the pews, re-carpeting, and then getting everything back in place in time for Easter Sunday.

Aside from keeping the literal doors of the church open, Art also sought to keep the church, and even his own home, open to all different kinds of people, so that everyone could have enough to eat, a steady job, and know God's love. When a young African-American man was hired at IBM in the 1960's, Art heard that this guy couldn't get a car loan without someone co-signing, and he was willing to do it without a second thought. While others at work struggled with integration in the workplace, Art and Dorothy would have this friend over to their home for dinner. When First Presbyterian was looking to hire a full-time custodian, Art went to bat for a former German soldier and prisoner of war (something not everyone on the committee was comfortable with). Art became very close to Walter and Frieda as they acclimated to becoming Americans. When Art and Dorothy's son Bruce brought a couple college friends home one weekend (who happened to be Jewish and Muslim) in the 1950's, Art's only concern was making sure they served the right foods that everyone could eat. They said it was a United Nations sleepover! When Dorothy's oldest sister lost her husband in the 1970's, Art made sure that Aunt Gladys was taken care of (home repairs, maintenance, and things like that), but more importantly that she was included in everything they did, even, eventually on Art and Dorothy's 50th anniversary trip to Alaska. Never one to close a door on anyone, truly, a doorkeeper in the house of the Lord.

Art and Dorothy raised their kids, and were thrilled to welcome grandkids, and great grandkids, as they eventually retired back to PA, and then finally down here to Clearwater. Art continued his "door keeping" responsibilities, serving on Trustees, or with the Ushers, at his church in Hartford, and then eventually here at Skycrest United Methodist Church.

Which brings me to a couple months ago, July 1st, when visiting Art became my first official pastoral duty at Skycrest United Methodist Church. That day, and every time I saw him after that, I want you all to know that he was so proud of each and every child, grandchild, great-grandchild. I have heard, sometimes even as Art struggled with pain as he spoke, about the careers, sports, activities, and accomplishments of each member of his family. Every time we spoke, he'd go over each branch of the family, who did what, whose kids were whose, and what he was proud of in each and every one of you.

And, then, he always talked to me about his beloved wife, best girl, Dorothy. His main concern in every visit was that I'd also stop by to see her. He insisted on reminding me of the room number, making sure that would be my next stop when I left his room. As we got to know each other more, he'd share with me about his sadness that Dorothy could no longer remember or converse, at least in a logical way, like she used to. But we agreed, and I always reminded him, that the most important thing was that she was always able to feel and to sense how much he loved her. After an amazing 75 years of marriage, I think some things can go unsaid, and still be, in a way, known. It seemed as if Art was ready to pass through the doors into God's eternal kingdom, but part of him wanted to keep holding that door open for Dorothy, all the way to the end.

The good news is that Jesus' gift to us, Jesus' death and resurrection, is a door that is flung wide open, to God's kingdom. The New Testament tells us that when Jesus died, the temple curtain, the one that kept the holiest part blocked off except to one guy once a year, that curtain was torn in two. We have a God, through Jesus Christ, who wants to be near to each of us, in our hearts, and with us forever in heaven.

Art has entered the final door. And he has inspired us with his life of door-keeping, door-opening, for others. And now as we open our hearts to Jesus, he will give us comfort in our time of grief, peace even as we face this loss, and the assurance that we, too, can enter that final door someday and rejoice eternally with Art and so many others, singing, "How lovely is your dwelling place, God! Better is one day in your courts than thousands elsewhere."

Thanks be to God.

Amen.

www.ingramcontent.com/pod-product-compliance
Lightning Source LLC
Chambersburg PA
CBHW052148110526
44591CB00012B/1897